Risicato's Sicilian Cookery

Giovanni Verga's Vizzini

Risicato's Sicilian Cookery

GIUSEPPE and PALMINA RISICATO

with

CHRISTINE MANGALA

and

DAVID FROST

Illustrated with Original Paintings and Drawings by

GIUSEPPE RISICATO

AQUILA

CAMBRIDGE • SYDNEY

Risicato's Sicilian Cookery

First published in 1998 by

Aquila Books (Australia)
49 Gladstone Street, Enmore, New South Wales 2042
Telephone & Fax: (02) 9550 1495
E-mail: aquilabk@ozemail.com.au

an associate of

Aquila Books Limited
(Registered in England No. 2490544)
Aquila House, 19 Ferry Path, Cambridge CB4 1HB, United Kingdom
Telephone & Fax: (01223) 323830 / 503023
E-mail: aquilabooks@compuserve.com

distributed in Australia by

Mind Mint Distributors
6 Fortune Street, Scarborough, Queensland 4020
Telephone: (07) 3880 0014, Fax: (07) 3880 0155

© text: Giuseppe Risicato, Palmina Risicato, Christine Mangala, David Frost, 1998
paintings and line-drawings: Giuseppe Risicato, 1980, 1998
photographs: Giuseppe Risicato (throughout); John Graham (p.34), Tom Davies
(p.85) from an original by Giuseppe Risicato, 1998

**This publication is copyright. No part of it may be reproduced, stored in a retrieval system
or transmitted without the written permission of the publishers.**

*The publishers wish to thank the following for permission to reproduce paintings in their possession:
Archbishop Gibran and the Australian Antiochian Church ('Mandalion'),
Mrs Kamala Desilva ('Ancestral Stones'), Professor David Frost ('Vizzini Streetscape'),
Joe and Sonia Ghabrial ('Rooftops of Vizzini' and 'A Venetian Lady'),
Palmina Risicato ('Gates').
The remaining paintings are from the artist's collection.*

Text: Christine Mangala with David Frost
Design and typesetting: David Frost
Consultant for Italian: Meera Frost

Printed in Hong Kong by South China Printing Co. (1988) Ltd

ISBN 0 9586613 2 4

Introduction

David Frost

This book offers typical Sicilian cookery. It is not typical of Sicily's rich regional variety (you won't find recipes from every corner of the island), and it does not represent the high and the low of Sicilian society (there is probably not much here that the nobs would admit to enjoying). But it is typical of an ordinary but proud Sicilian family from the small town of Vizzini, near to Catania, on the eastern side—and probably typical only of the Risicato side of the street.

Of course, it is rather more than that, because one of our two contributors, Giuseppe Risicato, has been for twenty years a restaurateur in the Hunter Valley region of New South Wales. Giuseppe is more than a lover of food: he came to Australia as a restorer of religious art, then did a variety of creative things, running a photographic studio and acting as official photographer to the 'Miss Australia' contest, conducting schools of deportment in Maitland and Sydney, doing interior designs for restaurants and hotels—and all the time painting and drawing, exhibiting as he moved about Australia. As his paintings of his home town of Vizzini enrich this book, so his creative gifts have enhanced the cooking he learned at his mother's knee. On occasions, we offer you what the Risicato family might serve for that special someone on their name-day, or for one of the many festivals that enliven Sicilian society.

Because the Risicatos are humble folk—Giuseppe's and his sister Palmina's forebears were tailors, shoemakers, barbers and the like—this is authentic everyday cooking, using modest and relatively inexpensive ingredients. Sicilians have been cooking for 10,000 years, and successive domination by the Greeks, the Romans, the Byzantines, the Arabs, the Normans, and the Bourbons must have added some international flavour; but this is the cuisine of a people who have been the football at the toe of Italy, fought over and kicked about for centuries, and still neglected by central government. So there isn't much scope for imported or exotic ingredients, and Giuseppe's recipes never use cream.

If spices and rich, heavy sauces are not a feature of this cookery, it is nevertheless wonderfully tasty and healthy. It uses a lot of those fibre-filled beans so dear to dieticians—and we teach you the trick of preparing them so as to avoid flatulence. Much of the frying is done in olive oil—the very best form of fat. If the cooking is really a set of variations on ancient rural themes (Sicily's economy is still largely agricultural), traditional skills have produced a surprising variety in taste and texture.

Risicato's Sicilian Cookery

Our two contributors have taken different paths, and this is reflected in the style of what they do. Giuseppe has seen the world: after a traditional artist's apprenticeship to a master, one Professor Messina, Giuseppe went to the mainland, exhibited his paintings in Rome and Milan, then worked his way round France and Switzerland, often doing theatrical makeup to earn a crust, or painting postcards for tourists. He escaped conscription into the Axis armies in the Second World War by fleeing from town to town, and on one occasion was a step away from death when the Nazis lined up the local population in the town square and shot them one by one, till someone confessed to taking part in a partisan raid.

Palmina, on the other hand—she is 'Palmina' because she was born on Palm Sunday—came straight to Australia from Vizzini as a young woman, and her sphere has been largely domestic, working as a tailor in Sydney, caring devotedly for a close-knit family of brothers and sisters. She has kept alive the subtler nuances of

Vincenzo Bellini of Catania

Introduction

domestic cooking. It is Palmina who dips her hands in white wine before she rolls her meat-patties. It is Palmina who remembers what was traditionally eaten by the family at the Feast of San Gregorio (page 85). Her recipes are delicate, carefully adjusted, where her brother's are masculine, bold, perhaps a bit brash—Giuseppe's 'Macco' (page 9), you might say, is a shade macho.

Sicily, if it has been a football for Europe, has also been the hub of the Mediterranean wheel, a melting-pot for more than a dozen ethnic groups, a centre of trade, and a prize to be captured. In consequence, Sicilians are an experienced, cultured race. The Greeks built them their first theatre, at Taormina (page 87), in the shadow of Europe's highest active volcano, Mount Etna. But if Sicilians erupt, they do it in song: the Italian popular song is thought to have originated in Sicily, and Sicily is famed for its lyric poetry. They are also natural dramatists: witness not just the festivals and processions (page 84) that grace Sicilian religious life, and the puppet shows that are a delight at local occasions, but also the contribution to world theatre of writers such as Luigi Pirandello. Drama and lyricism combine in the operas of Vincenzo Bellini from Catania and of Piero Mascagni—works that are heard well-nigh every night in the opera-houses of the world. Mascagni, of course, took the plot of his Cavalleria Rusticana *from a story by Giovanni Verga, who with his fellow Sicilian Leonardo Sciascia, is among Italy's most distinguished modern writers—and* Cavalleria Rusticana, *naturally, is set in Verga's home town of Vizzini. How then could Giuseppe not celebrate his people's love of the arts by special recipes honouring the renaissance painter Antonello da Messina (page 101), the composer Bellini (page 73), the novelist Verga (and that writer's passion for rabbit, which he indulged each year with his friend, maestro Mascagni (page 75))?*

This then is a book from a people who not only care about food, but for whom food is an important element in a rich cultural life. You may have to prepare it simply and quickly (quite a few of our recipes are economical not just of money but of time); but food is something to be savoured and not rushed through, something to be talked about and talked over. Giuseppe and Palmina care about the quality of its ingredients as Giuseppe cares about the paints on his palette. The two of them are the terror of shopkeepers: Palmina looking a sardine in the eye and flank to assess its freshness; Giuseppe weighing mussels in the hand to ensure they are both weighty and closed. We pass on their tips: how to cook your potatoes in the steam (and with the flavour) of the main dish; how to boil your calamari *so it won't end up about as chewsome as rubber-bands. Even in Sicily, mountainous except for the fertile plain of Catania, beautiful and still largely unspoilt, modern life is killing traditions. We capture those traditions here, so they can be handed on to another generation.*

Risicato's Sicilian Cookery

Sunday

Introduction

The Sicilian Store Cupboard

We have listed here the items that it would be most helpful to keep in your store cupboard if you are intending to make regular use of our Sicilian Cookery. *Since we offer family cooking, neither hoity-toity nor frenchified, the ingredients are simple and inexpensive. Nevertheless, subtle and delicious dishes can be created from them: the secret lies in preparation and cooking. As most of our store cupboard items are budget-priced, you might be able to keep to hand a bottle or two of wine and some liqueurs. It is amazing how a dash of Cinzano or a glass of white wine (introduced, of course, when instructed) will transform an unpretentious dish into something special.*

Olive oil is, naturally, ideal for Sicilian cooking; but should you find it a touch expensive, it is permissible to mix olive oil with vegetable oil except *in those recipes where olive oil is specified.*

As for herbs, these should always be fresh, especially basil and parsley. It is possible to use dried oregano, and you might just get away with dried rosemary. For the rest— don't even think of it!

CONTENTS

PASTA	spaghetti, linguine, tagliatelle, penne, farfalle, lasagna, pastina, risoni
RICE	the short-grained variety
DRIED BEANS	fave (broad beans), fagioli *(otherwise 'kidney beans' or 'borlotti beans')*, black-eyed beans, brown lentils, chickpeas
TOMATOES	tins of peeled, ripe tomatoes *(preferably Italian)*
TUNA	tins of quality tuna in oil
ANCHOVIES	jars of anchovies *(not tins)*
OLIVES	plain green olives, black olives
CHEESE	a block of hard pecorino *or* of parmesan *(Giuseppe prefers to use pecorino, but that is a personal preference)*
OIL	olive oil, vegetable oil
VINEGAR	a good wine vinegar
HERBS	basil, mint, parsley, rosemary; oregano, fresh or dried
WINES	red and white wine, marsala
LIQUEURS	Galliano, sambuca
VERMOUTH	Cinzano

A Table of Equivalent Weights and Measures

All the measurements in this book are metric, and the measures of cup, teaspoon and tablespoon conform to those approved by Standards Australia (1 cup = 250 ml, 1 tablespoon = 20 ml, 1 teaspoon = 5 ml). In the United Kingdom, the United States, New Zealand and Canada, a tablespoon = 15 ml. All cup and spoon measurements are level, and dry ingredients should be shaken loosely and not packed down.

The table below gives approximate equivalents of metric measures. The difference beween an approximate and an exact equivalent is slight, and will not affect your results. It is easy to convert our metric measures into imperial; and you may take heart from the fact that Giuseppe and Palmina Risicato, like most experienced cooks, do not measure out their ingredients but work by instinct. Follow your own good sense, and all will be well.

DRY MEASURES

METRIC	IMPERIAL
15 g	½ oz
30 g	1 oz
60 g	2 oz
90 g	3 oz
125 g	4 oz (¼ lb)
155 g	5 oz
185 g	6 oz
220 g	7 oz
250 g	8 oz (½ lb)
280 g	9 oz
315 g	10 oz
345 g	11 oz
410 g	12 oz (¾ lb)
440 g	14 oz
470 g	15 oz
500 g	16 oz
750 g	24 oz (1½ lb)
1 kilo	32 oz (2 lb)

LIQUID MEASURES

METRIC	IMPERIAL
30 ml	1 fluid oz
60 ml	2 fluid oz
100 ml	3 fluid oz
125 ml	4 fluid oz
150 ml	5 fluid oz (¼ pint)
190 ml	6 fluid oz
250 ml	8 fluid oz
300 ml	10 fluid oz (½ pint)
500 ml	16 fluid oz
600 ml	20 fluid oz (1 pint)
1 litre	(1¾ pints)

MEASURES OF LENGTH

1 cm is roughly ½ in
2 cm are nearer ¾ in
5 cm approximate to 2in
10 cm are roughly 4 in
20 cm are about 8 in

OVEN TEMPERATURES

OUR TERM	C (Centigrade or Celsius)	F (Fahrenheit)	GAS MARK
Low	150	300	2
Medium	180 – 190	350 – 375	4
Medium hot	200 – 210	400 – 425	5
Hot	220 – 230	450 – 475	6
Very hot	240 – 250	500 – 525	7

SOUPS

Wash-Day in Vizzini

Serves 6 – 8

Palmina's Potato Soup

INGREDIENTS

6 potatoes, peeled
4 tomatoes
½ cup of parsley, chopped
1 cup of risoni (rice-shaped) pasta
1 bowl of grated pecorino cheese

2 onions, roughly chopped
6 tablespoons of oil
4 pieces of celery, chopped
(from the tender white part)
salt and pepper

Scald the tomatoes in boiling water, peel off their skins, and chop. Slice the potatoes. Heat five tablespoons of oil in a saucepan and put in the chopped onions, with half a tablespoon of salt. Cook over a medium heat for ten minutes. Add half the chopped parsley and tomatoes, and cook for a further ten minutes. Add the celery, with three cups of water.

In a frypan, sauté the potatoes in one tablespoon of oil. Sprinkle some chopped parsley. Cook for five minutes, then add to the saucepan. Turn the heat down and cook slowly for half an hour.

Cook the *risoni* in boiling water for twenty minutes. Add two cups of water to the soup and put in the cooked pasta. Adjust your salt, then sprinkle the rest of the chopped parsley. Serve with a little cheese sprinkled over, or hand round the bowl of cheese.

Serves 6 – 8

Minestra coi piselli: Palmina's Pea Soup

INGREDIENTS

1 kilo of frozen baby peas
2 onions, finely chopped
200 g of peeled tomatoes
2 tablespoons of grated pecorino
salt and pepper

2 potatoes, peeled and chopped
2 teaspoons of chopped garlic
4 tablespoons of oil
125 g of pastina

Place the frozen peas in a bowl of hot water for fifteen minutes, and then drain. Heat oil in a heavy saucepan, and cook the onions in it till they turn golden. Add the peas, with two teaspoons of chopped garlic, and salt. Cook for three minutes.

Break and mash tomatoes with a spoon, then add them to the saucepan. Put in pepper, two tablespoons of grated pecorino, and one litre of water. Cover and cook slowly for half an hour. Add chopped potatoes and cook for another half hour, adding a little water if needed. Cook 125 grams of *pastina* in salted boiling water, drain, and add to the soup.

Soups

Serves 8

'Macco':
Purée of Broad Beans

'Macco' is a staple food in Sicily, full of iron and goodness. Children are urged to eat it so that they may grow strong. It is thought to be especially good in bad weather.

> INGREDIENTS
> **500 g of fave (dried broad) beans**
> *(washed several times and soaked overnight)*
>
> **2 medium size onions**
> **4 cloves of garlic, chopped**
> **2 or 3 sticks of celery**
> *(preferably the tender inner parts, with leaves chopped fine)*
>
> **a fistful of linguine or thin spaghetti**, broken up
> **2 tablespoons of cooking oil**
> **2 tablespoons of olive oil**
> **3 tablespoons of grated pecorino**
> **1 cup of chopped parsley**
> **salt and pepper**

Remove from the soaked beans their brown skins. Put the beans in a large saucepan with plenty of water. Add salt. Bring to the boil and simmer for twenty to thirty minutes until the beans go soft and can be mashed with a fork. Drain the beans, keeping the broth. Mash them thoroughly, and return to the saucepan with the broth.

Heat oil in a frypan. Add onions and garlic and soften on a low heat, keeping the pan covered. Add softened onion, garlic and celery to the saucepan. Sprinkle chopped parsley, and cook for another ten minutes.

Add the spaghetti pieces and cook until they are soft but firm. Drizzle olive oil, then sprinkle with pecorino. Season with pepper, and adjust the salt if necessary.

The *macco* should be the consistency of a purée but may be thinned to serve as soup.

Distant Towers

Soups

Serves 8 – 10

Lentil Soup—Vegetarian

INGREDIENTS
500 g of brown lentils
400 g of tinned tomatoes
2 onions, chopped
1 tablespoon of chopped garlic
2 tablespoons of oil
3 sticks of celery
(*4 inches long, taken from the leafy end*)
2 carrots, scraped and chopped
2 litres of water
4 tablespoons of olive oil
salt

Heat the oil in a large saucepan. Put in the onions and garlic, and soften them on a low heat. Add the tomatoes and cook slowly for five to seven minutes. Add the chopped carrots, and cook slowly for another five minutes.

Add two litres of water and bring to the boil. Put the lentils in. Chop the leafy ends of celery and add. Bring to the boil again, and keep on the boil for about fifteen minutes. Lower heat, cover, and cook for another hour, or until the lentils are well-cooked. Add salt.

Serve in bowls, and spoon a teaspoon of olive oil over each bowl.

Lentil Soup—Non-Vegetarian

INGREDIENTS
as above, plus
4 lamb shanks

Proceed as above. Add four lamb shanks when you put the lentils in. When lentils and meat are done, you may prefer to remove the bones, cut up the meat and return it to the soup.

A Wall in Vizzini

Soups

Serves 6

Three-in-One Winter Fare
Fagioli conditi—Minestrone—Zampe di maiale

This is a very versatile and economical dish for the cold weather. You can use the soup with pasta as a full meal at night, and the fagioli conditi *with crusty bread as a light, cold lunch or supper. Those who cannot face the sight of pig's trotters on a plate may still enjoy the soup.*

The main ingredient for all three dishes is **a kilo of pale pink dried fagioli (borlotti beans)**, which need to be soaked overnight. Cook in a large saucepan in salted water for an hour, or until the beans go soft when pressed. Take out three cups for the *antipasto*, continue cooking the remainder.

Antipasto: Fagioli conditi	*Minestrone and Main Course*
INGREDIENTS	INGREDIENTS
1 tender marrow (cucuzza)	*6 pig's trotters*
6 tablespoons of oil	*2 sticks of celery*, chopped
2 tablespoons of chopped garlic	*2 tomatoes*, chopped
3 tablespoons of white wine vinegar	*3 onions*, chopped, and softened
4 tablespoons of chopped parsley	slowly in *3 tablespoons of oil*
salt, and a pinch of oregano	*2 tablespoons of olive oil*
for decoration	*a few leaves of basil*
tender sticks of celery	*1 cup of cooked pasta* (optional)
12 kalamata olives	*some plain boiled potatoes*
sliced cucumber	*salt and pepper*
slivers of roasted red peppers (see page 98)	

Antipasto Cut the *cucuzza* in thick slices. Fry gently in oil on a low heat. Add chopped garlic, salt, oregano, vinegar, and parsley. Pile three cups of cooked *fagioli* on a platter, and decorate with *cucuzza*, olives, cucumber, celery, and roasted red pepper slivers.

Minestrone Add to the pot of *fagioli* the pig's trotters, the softened onions, celery, chopped tomatoes, one teaspoon of salt, pepper, and basil, and cook for another hour. Take out the pig's trotters and set them aside. Drizzle olive oil over the soup, and serve it with or without the cooked pasta.

Main Course Serve the pig's trotters with boiled potatoes to those of the family who are neither squeamish nor satisfied by what has gone before.

Serves 10 – 12

Minestra di ceci: Chickpea Soup

INGREDIENTS

1 kilo of dried chickpeas, soaked overnight
6 celery sticks (the white and tender parts), chopped
salt
3 onions, chopped fine
1 cup of chopped parsley
½ cup of oil
2 tablespoons of Napoletana sauce
pepper

Rinse the chickpeas three times. Put them in a saucepan with plenty of water, enough to cover and with at least six centimetres clear above. Bring to the boil, and remove any white scum as it rises to the top.

In a frypan, soften the onions in oil over a medium heat. Add them to the chickpeas, along with the chopped celery and parsley. Cook slowly for one hour, then add one and a half tablespoons of salt, a pinch of pepper, and the Napoletana sauce (see page 21). Cook a little more, then test to make sure the peas are soft. Adjust your salt and serve.

Serves 6 – 8

Minestra con fave fresche:
Soup with Broad Beans

INGREDIENTS

500 g of frozen broad beans (the small variety)
2 sticks of celery (the tender, white, leafy part)
2 tablespoons of grated pecorino
salt
2 teaspoons of chopped garlic
2 onions, finely chopped
2 fresh tomatoes
4 tablespoons of oil
125 g of pastina (optional)
pepper

If fresh broad beans are in season, peel enough pods to get five hundred grams of beans. If the beans are frozen, put them in a bowl of hot water for fifteen minutes, then drain. Scald the tomatoes in boiling water, skin them and chop the flesh.

Heat the oil in a heavy saucepan, drop in the onions and cook on a low heat till they turn golden brown. Add the beans, garlic, one teaspoon of salt and a little pepper. Cook for three minutes, then add the tomatoes, diced celery, the pecorino, and one litre of water. Cover and cook slowly for half an hour. You may add cooked *pastina* just before serving.

Soups

Serves 6 – 8

Broccoli Soup

INGREDIENTS
2 large fresh tomatoes
½ cup of oil
1 tablespoon of grated pecorino
3 heads of broccoli
3 cloves of garlic, sliced
1 cup of alphabet-noodles
salt and pepper

Wash, trim and cut the broccoli into chunky florets. Peel stems, and cut up tender parts. Scald tomatoes in boiling water, peel the skins, and chop the flesh. Heat oil in a frypan and lightly fry the garlic-slices for three minutes. Add chopped tomatoes and half a teaspoon of salt. Cook for ten minutes, mashing the tomatoes to make a sauce. Set the frypan aside.

Bring three litres of water to the boil in a saucepan. Put in the broccoli, add a tablespoon of salt. Boil for ten minutes, until the broccoli are cooked but firm. Remove from the heat.

Put back your frypan with the tomato sauce. Take two or three florets from the water, and add them to the tomato sauce with a pinch of pepper. Heat them through for five minutes, breaking the broccoli up into small pieces. Remove from the heat.

Just before serving, bring the broccoli still in their water to the boil again and drop in the noodles, cooking them for seven minutes till they turn *al dente*. Add the tomato sauce and the grated pecorino cheese, mixing well. The soup is now ready to serve.

Serves 6 – 8

Minestra tutte le verdure e col vitello:
Mixed Vegetable Soup with Veal Chops

This is a hearty yet nourishing soup, a meal in itself. Use what you can get of peas, broad beans, spring onions, green beans, broccoli, carrots, celery, zucchini, spinach.

INGREDIENTS
3 onions
3 fresh tomatoes
6 veal chops (optional)
500 g of fresh mixed vegetables
1 tablespoon of chopped garlic
½ cup of oil
salt and pepper

Scald the tomatoes in boiling water. Peel off their skins and chop the flesh. Heat oil in a heavy saucepan and lightly brown the onions over a low heat. Put in the diced mixed vegetables, add a teaspoon of salt, then cover and cook, stirring now and then. Add the tomatoes and two litres of water. Cook for an hour. If you are using veal chops, fry them in a tablespoon of oil, and add to the soup. Serve with grated pecorino.

Mother and Child

Soups

Serves 6 – 8

Brodo di pollo: Chicken Soup

This soup is more than a soup: it can provide several different main meals. Its chicken and vegetables may be served later on their own, with additional vegetables, or with eggs in Napoletana sauce (see page 36). Or you may make a delicious spezzatino *with the left-over chicken (page 64). Spatchcock or pigeons may be used in place of chicken.*

INGREDIENTS
4 chicken legs
4 carrots, peeled and cut in half
4 sprigs of parsley
4 potatoes, peeled and halved
250 g of pastina (or small pasta)
salt

4 chicken thighs
4 sticks of celery
2 large onions, sliced
200 g of tomatoes
grated pecorino cheese
pepper

Put the chicken pieces with the celery, onions, parsley, carrots and tomatoes into a large saucepan. Add three litres of water. Bring to the boil, then turn the heat down.

Cook slowly, skimming off any fat and scum that rise to the top. After two hours, add the potatoes and cook for another twenty minutes. Remove chicken pieces, potatoes and other vegetables, keeping them warm for a main course.

Boil salted water in another pan, add the *pastina*, and cook for five minutes. Drain, add the *pastina* to the soup, and cook for another five minutes until the *pastina* is cooked through. Serve in bowls, sprinkling grated cheese over it.

Serves 6 – 8

Brodino: Soup with Meat-Balls

INGREDIENTS
250 g of minced veal
2 tablespoons of grated parmesan
½ cup of cooked rice
salt and pepper

4 eggs
2 tablespoons of chopped parsley
2 tablespoons of white wine
1 cup of pastina

Proceed as for the *brodo*, but do not add any *pastina*. Put veal in a bowl, with parmesan, parsley, and a pinch of salt and pepper. Addd two eggs and the cooked rice, a little at a time, and mix well. Use wine in a bowl to moisten your hands, and make small meat-balls. Drop them in the hot soup, and simmer for ten minutes. Remove meat-balls, chicken and vegetables with a slotted spoon. Cook a cup of *pastina* in another saucepan, add it to the soup with two beaten eggs. Return the meat-balls to the soup, and it is ready to serve.

Serves 6 – 8

Stracciatella di pesce:
Fish Soup

INGREDIENTS

1 head of blue-eyed cod (2 kg) or **other fish-heads of equal quality**
2 large onions, sliced
2 tablespoons of olive oil
chopped parsley
pepper
2 fresh tomatoes, chopped fine
2 eggs
salt

If fish is fresh, its eyes are bright and shiny. Wash the head thoroughly, cleaning out and discarding innards. Cut it in half and wash again. Soften your onions in oil in a large saucepan over a medium heat, but don't let them brown. Then put in the chopped tomatoes, and cook for ten minutes till you get a sauce. Pour in two litres of water, bring to the boil, and put in your fish-head. Add a teaspoon of salt and a pinch of pepper, and simmer for an hour and a half. Strain the broth into a fresh pan, discarding bones and any other remnants. Bring to the boil, then beat your eggs and add them, along with some chopped parsley. At this point, turn off the heat.

(You should note that this is definitely a *fish* soup. If the flavour is too robust, you may dilute to taste by adding a little more hot water.)

Serves 6

Zuppa alla marinara: Seafood Soup

This recipe can be made with mussels and prawns alone, or with a mix of fresh mussels, crab, balmain bugs, pippi, vongole and green prawns.

INGREDIENTS

2 kilo of fresh shellfish, including mussels and prawns
400 g of tinned tomatoes
2 onions, chopped fine
chopped parsley
4 tablespoons of chopped garlic
3 tablespoons of oil
salt and pepper

Wash and clean the seafood thoroughly (instructions are on page 42). Heat your oil, then add garlic and onions. Cook for three minutes on a low heat, add the tomatoes and all the shellfish except the prawns. Mix well, and cook for fifteen minutes. When the tomatoes are pulped and the shells of the seafood have opened, add the prawns. Once they turn pink, the dish can be removed from the heat and served.

PASTA, PIZZA, RISOTTO,

'What's for Dinner?'

FRITTATA and SAUCES

Cooking Pasta

Pasta has become such familiar food that it hardly needs any introduction. Nevertheless, to get the best results from cooking pasta a few tips may be useful.

Always use a large saucepan with plenty of salted boiling water, to which a tablespoon of oil may be added.

Long, thin pasta such as spaghetti, linguine, fettucine, tagliatelle *may need eight to twelve minutes of boiling to get the soft yet chewy* al dente *texture.* Maccheroni *(macaroni) and* tortellini *take a little longer. Fine* vermicelli *needs careful cooking, since the surface goes soft quickly while the core takes longer.* Risoni *(rice-shaped) looks deceptively small, but needs a good twenty minutes.* Gnocchi, *on the other hand, though largish in size, needs no more than the time it takes the dumplings to rise to the surface of the boiling water.*

Lasagna and Cannelloni

Sauces

Sicilian sauces for pasta tend to be light, flavoursome and healthy, since they shun cream. Besides making specific sauces for pasta, Sicilians use juices from a main-course dish to flavour pasta: for instance, Spaghetti in bianco *is a supplementary first course made from* Chicken Siciliana *(see page 57). Sauces from other baked dishes may be similarly used.*

The sauces given below are versatile. They may be used to make risotto, *to flavour stuffings and* frittata. *Buon appetito!*

Napoletana Sauce

This popular tomato sauce is so often called for in Sicilian cookery that it is useful to have some in the fridge, ready-made. If using fresh tomatoes, scald them in boiling water and proceed as for the tinned variety.

INGREDIENTS
400 g of tinned tomatoes
1 tablespoon of oil
1 tablespoon of chopped garlic
a few fresh basil leaves
salt
1 teaspoon of sugar (optional)

Heat oil in a pan, add the chopped garlic, and cook a little to soften the garlic. Add the tomatoes, one teaspoon of salt and one of sugar, and mash with a ladle as it cooks. Cook slowly for fifteen to twenty minutes, then add the basil leaves.

Bolognese Sauce

INGREDIENTS
250 g of minced veal
250 g of minced beef
2 tins of tomatoes (400 g each)
1 tablespoon of chopped garlic
salt
pepper
3 tablespoons of oil

Heat three tablespoons of oil in a saucepan. Put in one tablespoon of chopped garlic, and soften. Add the meat, and stir well until it turns brown. Add the two tins of tomatoes, three teaspoons of salt, and a little pepper. Cook slowly for an hour, stirring now and then.

Broccoli and Tomato Sauce

INGREDIENTS
400 g of tomatoes
2 tablespoons of chopped garlic
4 tablespoons of grated pecorino
2 heads of broccoli
salt
5 tablespoons of oil

Make Napoletana sauce, using a tablespoon of garlic, one tablespoon of oil and four hundred grams of tomatoes (see page 21).

Cut off the hard ends of the broccoli and discard. Slice the florets and the tender part of their stem into quarters. Wash, and place in a large saucepan. Cover with water and add a teaspoon of salt. Bring to the boil, and boil slowly for about eight to ten minutes. Drain.

Heat two tablespoons of oil in a frypan. Put in the garlic and broccoli and add half the Napoletana sauce, reserving the rest for pouring over your pasta. Stir in the cheese and cook for three to five minutes.

Mix the broccoli chunks with your cooked pasta, pour the pan-juices over, and stir in the Napoletana sauce.

Aglio-Olio:
Garlic and Olive Oil Sauce

INGREDIENTS
2 large, ripe tomatoes
½ cup of grated pecorino
500 g of *spaghetti* or *linguine*
some fresh basil leaves
3 tablespoons of chopped garlic
1 cup of olive oil
salt

Scald the tomatoes in boiling water. Peel them, and chop them roughly. Tear the basil leaves. Put oil, garlic, tomatoes, basil, and half a teaspoon of salt into a shallow pan. Cook on a low heat for five to seven minutes, mashing the tomatoes. Don't let the garlic burn. When the tomatoes are cooked, add one third of a cup of cheese, a little at a time, and cook for another three to five minutes, until the cheese blends with the rest.*

Cook the spaghetti or the linguine in plenty of salted water. Drain, and arrange on a platter. Sprinkle the rest of the cheese over, and mix in the garlic sauce.

*Note
You may add a few anchovies to the sauce, but if you do so, it is wise to omit the salt.

Serves 8 – 10

Lasagna

This Sicilian version of one of the most popular Italian dishes is lighter and simpler than the heavily-sauced generic version one meets in restaurants or in the freezer-section of supermarkets.

There are four stages in the preparation of lasagna: (i) making Bolognese sauce; (ii) making Napoletana sauce; (iii) boiling the pasta-sheets; (iv) assembling the ingredients for baking.

> INGREDIENTS
> **Napoletana sauce made with 400 g of tomatoes** (see page 21)
> **Bolognese sauce made with 500 g of minced veal and beef** (see page 21)
> **24 sheets of lasagna-pasta**   **2 tablespoons of oil**
> **salt**   **500 g of finely grated pecorino**
> **500 g of shredded mozzarella**

Fill a large saucepan three-quarters-full of water. Add one teaspoon of salt and one tablespoon of oil. Bring the water to the boil. Drop in eight sheets of lasagna-pasta, and cook for ten to twelve minutes, turning the sheets gently to keep them separate. Make sure that the water does not go off the boil. Lift the cooked pasta-sheets, using a small colander, and place them in cold water, either in a clean stainless-steel sink or in a plastic bowl. When the pasta-sheets are cool enough to handle, lift them out, drain them, and set them aside. Repeat the process with the remainder of the pasta-sheets.

Spoon some Bolognese sauce into a deep rectangular baking-dish (approximately 34 cms by 27 cms by 5 cms). Spread the sauce over the whole surface. Place two sheets of pasta to cover the whole surface, adding an extra strip if necessary.

Spoon over the pasta two to three tablespoons of Bolognese sauce, spreading it evenly, sprinkle some pecorino, and over that some mozzarella. Place another layer of pasta and repeat the process till you have six layers. On the uppermost layer of pasta, pour four tablespoons of Napoletana sauce (no Bolognese sauce), and sprinkle mozzarella.

Place in a moderately heated oven for about fifteen minutes. When cooked, use a sharp, serrated knife to cut the lasagna into squares. Serve with a green salad.

Note: Lasagna can be frozen before the final baking. If you wish to re-heat leftover lasagna, it is best to turn over the top layer of pasta, sprinkle some mozzarella, and then heat the dish through in a moderate oven.

Serves 4 – 6

Seafood Lasagna

INGREDIENTS
375 g (12 sheets) of lasagna
1 kilo of marinara (seafood mix)
4 tablespoons of oil
4 cloves of garlic, sliced
1 cup of chopped parsley
3 tablespoons of Napoletana sauce (see page 21)
250 g of mozzarella cheese, shredded
salt and pepper

Cook the lasagna-sheets in salted boiling water, following the method described on page 23. Cool the sheets and set them aside.

If the *marinara*-mix is frozen, thaw it out thoroughly. Then heat two tablespoons of oil in a frypan, and fry the garlic slices till they turn a pale brown. Add the *marinara*-mix, with one teaspoon of salt and a few twists of pepper. Mix in your Napoletana sauce (see page 21), but not too much of it: the idea is to end up with a sauce that is pale pink. Cover, and cook for ten minutes over a medium heat. Put in the chopped parsley, and mix-in two tablespoons of oil. Let it cool.

Cover the bottom of a baking-tin with lasagna-sheets. The tin should be roughly 25 by 26 centimetres by 5 centimetres. Spoon some of your *marinara*-mix over the sheets, about two to three tablespoons for each layer, spreading it evenly. Now sprinkle some shredded mozzarella. Lay on another layer of lasagna-sheets, and repeat the whole process till you have used up all your sheets. Sprinkle extra mozzarella on the topmost layer. Cover with foil.

Heat through in a medium oven for ten to fifteen minutes. You will find that the melted mozzarella holds the *marinara*-mix together.

A Note on Freezing
Normally, Giuseppe abhors the notion of freezing Sicilian food, because you lose the delicate natural flavours. However, once the seafood has been cooked, this lasagna stands up quite well to freezing, and even the maestro has been known to break his principles so as to be prepared for those occasional unexpected guests. Remember, though, that you *must* thaw out the lasagna slowly and thoroughly before re-heating.

Serves 4 – 6

Cannelloni

INGREDIENTS
Napoletana sauce made with 400 g of tinned tomatoes (see page 21)

12 lasagna pasta-sheets
125 g of minced pork
2 eggs
4 tablespoons of breadcrumbs
salt

125 g of minced veal
1 tablespoon of chopped garlic
4 tablespoons of grated pecorino
1 tablespoon of chopped parsley
pepper

Place the minced veal, the minced pork, garlic, pecorino and breadcrumbs in a bowl, and add two teaspoons of salt and a pinch of pepper. Break in the eggs, and mix well. Cook the meat slowly in a frypan for about twenty minutes, then set aside to cool.

Cook the pasta-sheets in plenty of salted water for ten to twelve minutes (as for lasagna). Rinse, and cool.

Spread out one sheet and cut it down to about seventeen centimetres in length. (The left-over strips may be cooked as *pappardelle* pasta, a thin, wide pasta which is particularly valued for its delicate texture when cooked in water or a broth and served with cut-up meat, especially hare).

Take three tablespoons of the cooked meat, and shape into a sausage long enough to fit the width of the pasta-sheet. Place it on one edge, and roll the pasta over to make a tight tube round it. Repeat till all the meat is used up. The meat mix should be adequate to make twelve *cannelloni*.

Place the *cannelloni* in a baking-dish, and spoon over them four to six tablespoons of Napoletana sauce. Sprinkle chopped parsley.

Bake in a moderately hot oven for fifteen minutes. Serve with a green salad.

Note
There is another excellent *canelloni* recipe on page 39, for *Spinach and Ricotta Cannelloni*.

Spaghetti con le seppie:
Black Spaghetti with Cuttlefish

Serves 8 – 10

Spaghetti con le seppie:
Black Spaghetti with Cuttlefish

INGREDIENTS
5 cuttlefish   *500 g of spaghetti*
½ glass of white wine   *salt*

Napoletana sauce (see page 21), made with
400 g of tomatoes   *a tablespoon of garlic*

Cleaning cuttlefish is a tricky operation but well worth the effort. Remove the bone, turn the tube inside out, and remove the head and tentacles. Wash the tube in cold water, scraping off the blue lining. Wash till the cuttlefish come white, then cut them into strips and set aside.

To clean the heads, remove any gristle on the sides, take out the eyes, and discard them. Carefully remove the ink-sacs and put them in a glass. Add white wine to them and set aside. Pick off any eggs after the ink-sacs have been removed, and discard.

The head and tentacles of a cuttlefish are tougher than its tube, so they need to be cooked separately. If the tube-strips are cooked along with the rest, they become tough, rubbery and inedible. To avoid this, bring water to boil in a saucepan, then drop in your tube-strips; turn off the heat and take them out. One second in boiling-hot water is sufficient to cook the tubes.

To cook heads and tentacles, on the other hand, you must fill a saucepan half-full with water, add salt, and bring it to the boil. Drop in heads and tentacles, and boil gently for fifteen minutes. Take the saucepan off the heat and let the cuttlefish cool in its stock.

Heat your Napoletana sauce in a frypan (instructions for making the sauce are on page 21). Pierce the ink-sacs in the wine, mix, and add four tablespoons of the ink to the Napoletana sauce.

Cook the spaghetti in salted and boiling water. Drain it, and pile in a bowl or platter. Pour the sauce over the whole, and mix well. Cut the tentacles in half, and decorate the spaghetti with tentacles and tubes.

Note
Another fine recipe for spaghetti with seafood is found on page 44, *Spaghetti Marinara*.

Risicato's Sicilian Cookery

Pasta with Fennel and Walnut

Serves 6 – 8

Pasta with Fennel and Walnut

INGREDIENTS

500 g of spaghetti **or** *linguine*
1 cup of walnuts
40 g of fennel herb (the feathery part)
3 tablespoons of oil
2 cups of breadcrumbs
salt and pepper
1 clove of garlic, chopped
2 tablespoons of olive oil

Sieve the breadcrumbs and crush the walnuts. Trim the fennel by removing its tough stalks.

Fill a large saucepan three-quarters full of water, adding a teaspoon of salt, and bring to the boil. Drop in the fennel and cook for half an hour.

Heat oil in a frypan, then add chopped garlic, breadcrumbs, half a teaspoon of salt and half a teaspoon of pepper. Keep stirring for about four minutes, till the breadcrumbs turn golden. Add your crushed walnuts, and stir well till the mixture turns to a rich brown. Be careful not to burn it.

When the fennel is cooked, drop in the pasta and boil rapidly for ten to fifteen minutes.

Test the pasta, and drain when cooked. Mix in olive oil, and turn it out into a serving-dish, and sprinkle walnut breadcrumbs over it.

Serves 4 – 6

Pasta with Artichokes

INGREDIENTS

250 g of artichokes
3 tablespoons of olive oil
grated pecorino
1 tablespoon of chopped garlic
200 g of Napoletana sauce

If the artichokes are fresh, remove their leaves and any hair from the heart. If they are tinned, drain the artichoke hearts. Heat oil, and lightly fry the garlic and artichoke hearts. Add Napoletana sauce (see page 21), and cook for five minutes. Pour the sauce over cooked pasta, and sprinkle cheese over the whole.

You may omit the Napoletana sauce and just served sautéed artichokes with a few twists of pepper, the grated cheese, and plenty of chopped parsley over the pasta.

Serves 6 – 8

Spaghetti alla Norma:
Spaghetti with Eggplant

The 'Norma' for whom this dish is named is not the restaurateur's wife, as so many visitors to Sicily must have imagined. Rather, she is the heroine of the last opera by Vincenzo Bellini, the great Sicilian-born composer whose portrait appears in our introduction (page 2). Nothing in the libretto suggests that Norma, High Priestess of the Druidic Temple, who led her people in revolt against their Roman oppressors, had a taste for this dish; but the coloratura soprano who created the role at La Scala and later at the first English performance at Covent Garden rejoiced in the name of Pasta, and perhaps that explains the connection.

Certainly, Sicilians take their opera seriously: as a mark of respect, either to heroine or to diva, Mama Risicato would prepare each serve individually rather than present just a haphazard mess in a platter.

INGREDIENTS
2 large, firm eggplants   oil for frying
500 g of fine spaghetti   lots of fresh basil
1 cup of grated pecorino   salt
Napoletana sauce made with **800 g of tinned tomatoes** *(see page 21)*

Peel and slice the eggplants lengthwise into thick slices. Drop them immediately into a bowl of salted water. Soak for an hour. Using a sharp knife lightly, remove any excess seeds from the surface. Dry the slices thoroughly. Heat oil in a frypan, put in two or three slices at a time, and fry on a medium heat for five minutes on each side until they turn soft inside and pale brown outside. Set aside.

Cook the spaghetti in plenty of salted, boiling water. Drain in a colander. Shred lots of basil and mix it into the spaghetti with half the Napoletana sauce.

Serving instructions
Put a ladleful of spaghetti on each dinner-plate. Place on it a slice of eggplant, dab a little sauce and sprinkle some cheese. Spoon over each portion another ladleful of spaghetti, a second slice of eggplant, then some more sauce and cheese. Top off each plate with some basil, and serve.

Serves 6 – 8

Capelli di angeli ed asparagi:
Asparagus and Angels' Hair

If you belong to the I-never-touch-pasta brigade, you may change your mind after sampling this dish. The pasta aptly called capelli di angeli *or 'Angels' Hair' makes for a delicate gradient of taste and texture that leaves one feeling light yet satisfied.*

INGREDIENTS
500 g of capelli di angeli
(sold as 'bird's nest' or 'vermicelli')
400 g of tinned tomatoes
2 tablespoons of olive oil
1 tablespoon of chopped parsley

3 bundles of asparagus
½ kilo of button mushrooms
200 g of tinned tuna
1 tablespoon of chopped garlic
salt

Cut about two inches off the tough end of the asparagus stems. Put these tough ends into a saucepan, pour one and a half cups of water over them, and boil slowly to make stock, for about twenty minutes.

Trim, wash and slice the mushrooms. Put mushrooms, chopped tuna and a little oil into a frypan. Add one teaspoon of salt and mix. Place the frypan on a low heat and cook with a lid over it, stirring frequently, for about ten minutes. Take four tablespoons of asparagus-stock from the saucepan, spoon it over the mushrooms, and cook for a little longer.

Put the tomatoes in another frypan, together with olive oil and garlic. Add one teaspoon of salt. Cook slowly for about fifteen minutes, mashing the tomatoes with a ladle. Add the rest of the asparagus-stock to the tomatoes. Place the asparagus-spears in the tomato-sauce, taking care not to break the buds. Cook slowly till the stems are tender yet still green.

To cook the 'bird's nest' or vermicelli
Put plenty of salted water in a large saucepan and bring to the boil. Put in the pasta, and bring back to the boil. Using a carving-fork, separate the strands. Cook for ten minutes, taking care not to let the water go off the boil. Because this pasta is fine, it goes soft quickly, so you need to make sure that it is cooked through. Drain it in a colander, running some cold water through it. Return it to the saucepan, add a little olive oil and warm through.

Pile the pasta on a dish. Pour over it juices from the mushroom-tuna mix, and also from the tomato and asparagus pan. Mix well. Place the asparagus-spears on top of the pile. Then surround the pasta with the mushroom-tuna mix, and sprinkle chopped parsley.

Gates

Pasta, Pizza, Risotto, Frittata, Sauces

Serves 6 – 8

Pizza and Inpannata

Pizza needs no introduction; inpannata *are closed pizzas, where the dough is folded over. This mixture will make two medium-size pizzas and four* inpannata.

INGREDIENTS
1 kg of plain flour
2 cm cube of fresh yeast
3 tablespoons of oil
salt

1 egg
1 cup of lukewarm water
3 teaspoons of sugar

Dissolve the yeast in one cup of lukewarm water. Pile the flour on a clean flat surface (a table-top or a marble slab). Make a well in the centre of the flour, and break in an egg. Add two teaspoons of salt, the liquid yeast, a little at a time, and mix well, rubbing the flour in fistfuls. Pour three tablespoons of oil over the dough as you mix it. Knead it with a rolling motion for about fifteen minutes until the surface shines smoothly. Shape the dough into a round, and wrap it in a tea-towel. Set it aside in a warm place for about twenty minutes until it starts to rise. Shape it into an oblong roll, then cut it across into six segments.

Beat each segment and shape it into a ball. Cover the segments with the tea-towel and leave them for thirty minutes in a warm place.

PIZZA INGREDIENTS
4 cloves of garlic,
finely chopped
2 tomatoes, finely chopped
anchovies

3 slices of pecorino cheese,
$1/2$ cm thick, cut into little cubes
3 tablespoons of oil
olives

Take a ball of dough and knead. Spread it out to make a circle, five millimetres thick. Oil a medium-sized pizza tin (about 25 cm across), and place the pizza dough-base on it. Using your fingertips, make indentations all over the surface. Pour one tablespoon of oil over the base and spread well. Place pieces of cubed cheese, tomato and garlic in the indentations, pressing them in. Decorate with anchovies. Bake in a hot oven for ten to fifteen minutes.

INPANNATA INGREDIENTS (4 servings)
2 bunches of spinach
4 heads of broccoli
5 tablespoons of oil
3 tablespoons of Napoletana sauce

salt
4 cups of water
4 tablespoons of chopped garlic
3 tablespoons of pecorino, grated

(see over)

Risicato's Sicilian Cookery

Bring two cups of water to the boil in a saucepan. Add one teaspoon of salt. Drop in washed spinach, let it wilt, and cook for five minutes. Using tongs or a slotted spoon, remove the spinach and set aside to cool. Add two more cups of water and one teaspoon of salt. Cut the stems off the broccoli and separate the florets. When the water boils, drop in the broccoli. Cover and cook for eight minutes. Do not overcook.

Heat two tablespoons of oil in a frypan. Fry two tablespoons of chopped garlic until it turns golden brown. Squeeze out excess water from the spinach, chop it, and put it in the frypan. Add two tablespoons of Napoletana sauce. Cook for five minutes, add a tablespoon of grated pecorino and stir well. Remove the spinach and set aside.

Add two more tablespoons of oil to the frypan, and fry two more tablespoons of garlic until it turns golden brown. Add the broccoli and one tablespoon of Napoletana sauce. Cook for eight minutes and add two tablespoons of grated pecorino. Stir well, then set aside.

Take a ball of dough, knead it flat and spread it out to form a circle, twenty-five centimetres in diameter and five millimetres thick. Put half the spinach on one half of the surface of the dough, fold the other half over and press down the edges. Brush with oil, then prick with a fork. Repeat the same process with the other three balls of dough, using up the rest of the spinach, and the broccoli. Place on a baking-tray and bake in a hot oven for ten to fifteen minutes, until they turn golden brown.

Serves 8

Risotto Risicato

Giuseppe's risotto is a quick, economical alternative to the traditional slowly-cooked risotto that is made with arborio *rice, which may not be available or affordable.*

INGREDIENTS
500 g of short-grain rice
2 x 185 g tins of tuna in oil
750 g of button mushrooms, sliced
3 tablespoons of chopped garlic
200 g of grated pecorino
500 g of baby peas

4 tablespoons of oil
400 g of tinned tomatoes
salt
1 teaspoon of sugar
250 ml of fresh chicken stock
a glass of white wine

To achieve a good flavour, you must have good chicken stock. To prepare stock, use either a chicken carcass from which all the meat has been picked, or four chicken wings. Boil carcass or wings in a litre of water, with an onion, carrot and celery. Strain the liquid off and add a glass of white wine.

Boil the rice in plenty of water. Drain, set aside. Heat two tablespoons of oil in a frypan. Put in two tablespoons of chopped garlic, let them soften, then add sliced mushrooms together with a teaspoon of salt, and cook for five to seven minutes. Remove and set aside.

Rinse your frypan, dry it, and put in the sliced onions with one tablespoon of oil. Cook them slowly for five minutes, or until they soften. Open one of the 185 gram tins of tuna, discard the oil, roughly chop the tuna, add it to the onions, and mix well.

Prepare Napoletana sauce (see page 21), using one 400 gram tin of tomatoes, one tablespoon of chopped garlic, and one tablespoon of oil.

Put the peas in a saucepan with enough water to cover, add a little salt and sugar, bring to the boil, then turn down the heat and simmer for five minutes. Drain and set aside.

Put the rice into a large mixing-bowl, add (a little at a time) half the mushrooms, half the cheese, the onions, and the second tin of tuna. Mix well, adding stock a little at a time to moisten the rice, which should be moist but not mushy. Add half the cooked peas and no more than two tablespoons of Napoletana sauce—the sauce should not dominate the risotto.

Arrange the risotto on a platter, alternating rice with peas. Top with mushrooms, sprinkle the rest of the cheese, then dab Napoletana sauce here and there to set off the peas.

Note: for a seafood risotto recipe, see *Risotto di pescatore* on page 44.

Serves 4

Eggs in Napoletana Sauce

This is a strikingly attractive and appetizing way to serve eggs, and is easily prepared in a few minutes, if you have Napoletana sauce already to hand.

Make Napoletana sauce in a frypan with 400 grams of tinned tomatoes (see page 21), or heat the sauce if already prepared. Once the sauce is ready, break four eggs into it, and let them set slowly over a low heat. When they are cooked, lift them out and serve with the sauce on hot buttered toast or with warm bread-rolls.

Serves 4

Frittata

INGREDIENTS
3 zucchini
4 eggs
1 tablespoon of chopped parsley
salt
slivers of roasted capsicum (optional)

1 onion, sliced
1 tablespoon of chopped garlic
3 tablespoons of grated pecorino
1 tablespoon of oil

Break the eggs in a bowl. Add chopped parsley, half the garlic, half a teaspoon of salt, and two tablespoons of pecorino. Beat lightly.

Wash, trim and slice the zucchini. Heat oil in a frypan and put in the onion slices. Turn the heat down. As the onion begins to soften, add the zucchini, the rest of the garlic, and half a teaspoon of salt. Cook for seven to ten minutes until the zucchini are cooked yet firm.

Pour the beaten eggs evenly over the surface of the vegetables, and cook on a very low heat for seven to ten minutes until the mixture sets.

Sprinkle the remainder of the pecorino over the *frittata*, and decorate with strips of roasted capsicum (for methods of roasting, see page 98).

A general note
Frittata is an adaptable dish. You can create tasty variations by following the above procedure, but using different vegetables: sautéed eggplants, capsicum, cooked and sautéed broccoli, or cooked spinach (see especially *Spinaci all' Antonello da Messina*, page 101). Leftover roast potatoes and chicken can also be sliced, diced, and treated in a similar way. A dash of Napoletana sauce always enhances flavour.

VERSATILE

Ricotta Street: Light and Shadow

RICOTTA

Versatile Ricotta

Ricotta cheese was originally (and to some ways of thinking, ideally) made with sheep's milk. Now, it is often made with cow's milk; but whatever the basic ingredient, it remains a light, refreshing cheese with a low-fat content and a creamy texture that makes it suitable for many a sweet or savoury dish.

In winter-time when Giuseppe was a boy, donkeys loaded with cones of ricotta were a familiar sight in Vizzini and its surrounding areas—in winter, because in summer the ricotta could not survive that mode of transport. Now, alas, the ricotta-donkeys are no more.

Ricotta is at its best when very fresh, so it is worth checking at your local delicatessen just when new supplies come in and if they come straight from the maker. When not entirely fresh, ricotta gets a yellowish tinge and a slightly bitter taste, and it is best to avoid it.

The versatility of ricotta is such that it can be used to make light snacks, substantial main meals, and the most delicate sweets. Cannoli di ricotta *is a crunchy but creamy sweet,* Cassata di ricotta *is a light, baked cheese-cake. Both are normally served on their own with wine and/or coffee.*

Serves 6 – 8

Penne with Ricotta

INGREDIENTS
500 g of penne pasta
¼ cup of water
2 tablespoons of grated pecorino
chopped parsley

3 cups of ricotta
3 tablespoons of Napoletana sauce
salt

Cook the *penne* in plenty of salted, boiling water. Drain, and put into a serving-bowl or platter.

Mix the ricotta with water in a bowl, until you get a creamy consistency. Pour it over the pasta, dab Napoletana sauce (see page 21), and sprinkle parsley.

Versatile Ricotta

Serves 4

Ricotta fritta

INGREDIENTS

1½ cups of ricotta
oil sufficient for shallow frying

Heat the oil in a frypan. Take a fistful of ricotta at a time, shape it into peach-sized balls, and put them in the oil. Cook gently over a medium heat for five minutes, then turn over with a spatula and fry for another five minutes. Serve while still warm.

Serves 4 – 6

Spinach and Ricotta Cannelloni

INGREDIENTS

8–10 lasagna pasta sheets (2 extra sheets, in case any break in cooking)
1 large bunch of Australian spinach or *2 bunches of English spinach*
3 cups of ricotta *½ cup of grated pecorino*
Napoletana sauce *1 tablespoon of oil*
made with 400 g of tomatoes *salt*

Cook the lasagna sheets in plenty of boiling water, in the manner described on page 23. Cool them in cold water and set aside.

Wash the spinach thoroughly — and then again! Remove the stems and tear the leaves roughly, then put them in a frypan with one tablespoon of oil and half a teaspoon of salt. Cook for ten minutes until the spinach is well done. Strain off any liquid and let the spinach cool. Take a fistful at a time and squeeze out all moisture. Place on a board and chop finely.

Mix your ricotta, spinach and a quarter of a cup of pecorino in a bowl. Divide the mix into eight portions. Cut two centimetres off the pasta-sheets so as to get an elegant shape (see page 23). Place one portion of ricotta-mix towards one edge of a pasta-sheet, sausage-fashion, and roll the sheet over firmly until you get a filled tube. Trim off any unfilled edges with a sharp knife.

Place the *cannelloni* in an oven-proof dish, and warm through in a medium-hot oven for five minutes. Put on to a serving-plate, dab some Napoletana sauce, and sprinkle pecorino. Extra sauce can be passed around, as required.

Makes 20

Cannoli di ricotta

INGREDIENTS

20 *cannoli-shells* (see page 106)*
1 cup of sugar
1 tablespoon of **Galliano** or **marsala**
3 cups of ricotta
1 teaspoon of vanilla essence
icing sugar (for dusting)

Mix ricotta, sugar, vanilla essence and liqueur in a bowl. Prepare a serving-plate by covering it in foil and dusting it with some icing sugar. Using a teaspoon, fill each *cannolo* with the ricotta-mix. With a knife, level off the filling at the open ends. Sprinkle some icing sugar over the *cannoli*, and serve.

*The method for making shells on page 106 is time-consuming, and excellent shells can be bought; so that in an emergency it is possible to make this sweet in ten minutes.

Serves 8

Cassata di ricotta

INGREDIENTS

30 g of butter
1 cup of sugar
2 cups of self-raising flour
1 tablespoon of Cinzano
3 cups of ricotta
3 tablespoons of **Galliano** or **marsala**
5 eggs

Melt the butter in a bowl placed over a saucepan of hot water. Mix ricotta in another bowl with half a cup of sugar and the liqueur.

Sieve the flour in a mixing-bowl, make a well, and break in three eggs. Break the remaining two eggs into another bowl. Remove the whites, beat the yolks lightly and set aside.

Put two tablespoons of sugar into the butter. Pour on to the eggs in the flour. Blend well to make a soft dough, using either a fork or an electric whisk. Take the dough out and knead it thoroughly for ten minutes, dusting your hands with a little flour.

Divide the dough into two rounds and roll each into a circle, half a centimetre thick. Grease two baking-trays and place the pastry-rounds on them. Divide your ricotta-mix into two and spread it evenly over each round. Brush with the beaten egg. Sprinkle a little sugar over each, then bake in a medium-hot oven for thirty minutes. When ready, it should have a meringue-like fluffy top and a spongy base. Always serve warm.

SEAFOOD

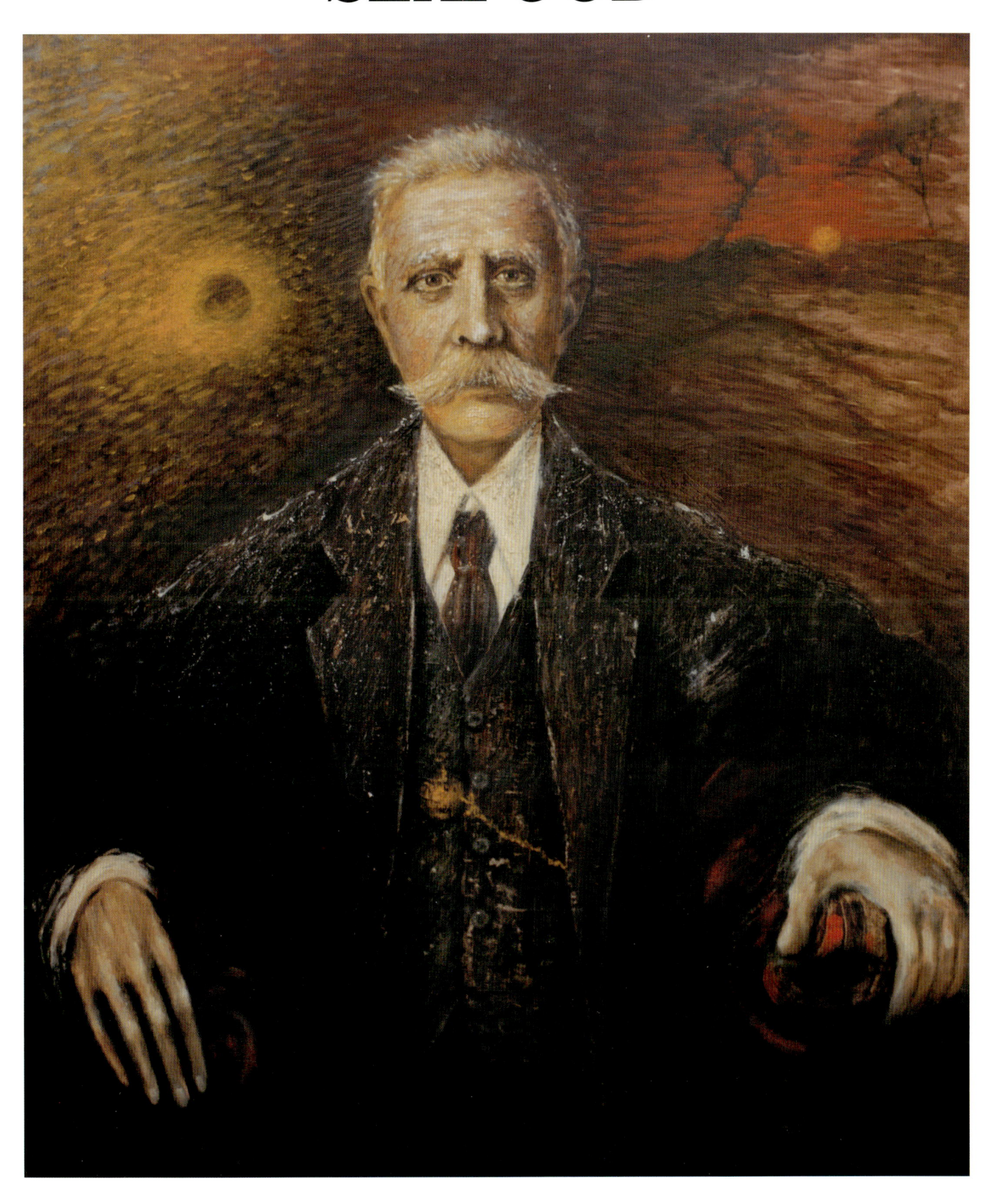

Dr Gesualdo Costa of Vizzini

The Preparation of Seafood
All seafood requires careful cleaning. Here are some tips.

To clean squid
Under running water, pull out the head and tentacles from the sac. Slip two fingers inside and gently remove small bones and spongy bits. Cut the head off. Remove and discard the dark gristle at the centre of the tentacles.

Using a serrated but not too sharp knife, scrape off the purple-blue skin. Wash thoroughly, and slice the white tube into rings one centimetre thick. Cut the tentacles across into halves, and trim any that are too long or spindly.

To clean octopus
Wash in plenty of water. Remove the eyes if they are still left in. Slit the sac with a sharp knife, and clean any grit from inside.

To clean prawns
Wash carefully, then cut off the heads. If you want to de-vein the prawns, a strong toothpick is ideal for the purpose. Insert its sharp end through the shell into the middle (the fleshiest part of the prawn), and hook the gut out crochet-fashion.

To clean mussels
Wash in plenty of water. Remove grit and fibre clinging to the shells.

Serves 6 – 8

Insalata di mare: Seafood Platter

If you have ever experienced eating squid or octopus that tasted like boiled rubberbands, it is understandable if you think ill of the seafoods themselves. But the fault, dear reader, lies not in the food but in the cooking. This delectable platter—octopus, squid, prawns and mussels—brings the riches of the sea to the table in a most appetising manner. The secret is to follow our very simple instructions. It may be served hot or cold, as an entrée or as a main course.

INGREDIENTS
1 kilo of squid	*½ kilo of cooked prawns*
1 kilo of octopus	*½ kilo of mussels in the shell*
3 lemons	*2 tablespoons of chopped garlic*
6 tablespoons of oil	*1½ glasses of white wine*
oregano	*parsley and lettuce leaves*
salt and pepper	*plenty of aluminium foil*

To cook octopus
Place the cleaned octopus in a large, oven-proof dish. Sprinkle one and a half teaspoons of salt, add a twist or two of pepper. Drizzle two teaspoons of oil and the juice of one lemon, sprinkle oregano, parsley, one tablespoon of chopped garlic, and add a generous glass of white wine. Cover the dish with foil, place in a medium hot oven and cook for about an hour. Test by cutting a bit from the toughest part. Adjust salt.

To cook squid
Place the tentacles and flaps in foil. Season with salt and pepper. Add the juice of half a lemon, two tablespoons of oil, oregano, parsley, a tablespoon of chopped garlic, and a little white wine. Make a tight parcel of it, using several layers of foil. Make the rings into another parcel in the same manner. Place them on a baking-tray, put in the hot oven, and cook for forty-five minutes.

The rings may be cooked on the stove. Place them in cold water, bring to the boil and immediately turn off the heat. Leave for a few minutes and take out. However, oven-baked squid are distinctly better in taste.

To cook mussels
Put them in a large saucepan with one cup of water (it is important to keep the water to a minimum). Cook slowly on a very low heat until the shells open.

Arrange octopus, squid, prawns and mussels on a bed of lettuce. Decorate with lemon slices.

Serves 8 – 10

Risotto di pescatore: Fisherman's Rice

How much seafood you use for this dish depends on your budget. If the same quantities are used as for the seafood platter, this dish can feed a large dinner party.

INGREDIENTS
fish as for the Seafood Platter (see page 43)
250 g of rice
2 tablespoons of chopped garlic
3 tablespoons of oil
½ kilo of marinara (seafood mix) (fresh or frozen)
salt and pepper
1 glass of wine
sprigs of parsley

Place the *marinara* or seafood-mix in a frypan. Add salt, pepper, garlic and wine. Cover with a lid, and cook slowly for twenty minutes. If you are using green prawns, these may be added to the pan in the last five minutes.

Cook 250 grams of rice, if possible using some of the broth from the pan that holds the seafood-mix.

Arrange the rice in a shallow dish. Pour over it the seafood-mix, with some of its juice. Mix well. Pile up the rice to make a mound. Decorate it with cooked octopus, squid, prawns, mussels, and a few sprigs of parsley.

Spaghetti alla marinara: Seafood Spaghetti

INGREDIENTS
fish as for the Seafood Platter (see page 43)
500 g of spaghetti or **linguine**
½ kilo of marinara (seafood mix) (fresh or frozen)

This popular dish is often marred by the addition of tomato sauce, which the seafood does not need.

Prepare as for the *Risotto di pescatore* (see above). Cook five hundred grams of spaghetti or *linguine*, mix into it the cooked seafood-mix, and decorate with cooked octopus, squid, mussels and prawns.

Note: another fine spaghetti and seafood recipe is found on page 27, *Spaghetti con le seppie (Spaghetti with Cuttlefish)*. See also *Seafood Lasagna* on page 24.

Seafood

Serves 4 – 6

Gamberi Costa: Brandied Prawns

Dr Costa was a well-loved physician in Vizzini, who ran his own hospital and was credited with saving many lives. He somehow managed to survive without collecting fees. It therefore seems appropriate that his portrait should introduce our inexpensive but healthy fish dishes (page 41). However, it must be admitted that Dr Costa's favourite breakfast was a biscuit, a cigar and a glass of cognac; so Giuseppe has named his brandied prawns in Dr Costa's honour. This dish is for that special occasion when you want to splash out and produce something exquisite, yet haven't much time or energy.

INGREDIENTS

750 g of large green prawns *125 ml of brandy*
1 tablespoon of oil *salt*

Wash the prawns thoroughly, strain them in a colander, and let them dry a little. Grease a frypan with a tablespoon of oil, and place the prawns in the pan with a pinch of salt. Spread them out evenly, then pour brandy all over. Mix them, and cook on a medium heat for a very short time, turning them constantly. As soon as they turn pink, take them off the heat or they will go hard.

Serve the prawns in their juice, which thickens naturally. Encourage your guests to suck out the heads of the prawns, as these are particularly flavoursome. Fresh breadrolls are essential for mopping up juices.

If you need to feed more people, you may fry garfish (see page 49), and surround them with the prawns.

Calamari ripieni: Stuffed Squid

Seafood

Serves 6

Calamari ripieni: Stuffed Squid

INGREDIENTS
6 squid
1 cup of cooked rice or leftover risotto
2 tablespoons of oil
2 tablespoons of chopped garlic
2 tablespoons of grated pecorino
2 tablespoons of chopped parsley
400 g of tomatoes
salt

Squid are slippery to handle when you try to stuff them, but they can easily be made manageable. Cut off the tentacles, chop them, and set aside. Wash the tubes and pat dry. Heat water in a saucepan till it is hot but not boiling. Drop in the squid-tubes, leaving them for only half a minute or less. As soon as they become oval, lift them out.

Heat a tablespoon of oil in a frypan, and put in the tentacles, a tablespoon of garlic, and one teaspoon of salt. Cook for five minutes. Add the rice, parsley and cheese, mixing well. When the mix is cool enough to handle, stuff the tubes with it.

Make Napoletana sauce in a frypan large enough to hold your stuffed squid. Heat one tablespoon of oil with one tablespoon of chopped garlic. As the garlic softens, add the tomatoes, and cook for fifteen minutes.

Place the stuffed squid in the pan of Napoletana sauce, spooning it over. Cover with a lid and cook slowly for seven minutes. Cut a small segment off the tapering end of the squid to see if it is cooked. Serve with the sauce and any leftover stuffing.

Serves 4

Calamari fritti: Fried Squid

INGREDIENTS
2 large squid
1 lemon
oil for frying
2 eggs
1 cup of flour
salt

Wash and clean the squid according to the instructions on page 42. Once cleaned, cut the tubes into rings, and the flaps and tender parts of the tentacles into strips.

Beat the eggs in a bowl. Pour flour on a plate, and dip the squid pieces, one at a time, first into egg, then into flour. Drop them in very hot (but not smoking) oil, and fry briefly. Take them out as they turn golden. Drain on kitchen-towels, sprinkle salt, and serve with a squeeze of lemon.

Risicato's Sicilian Cookery

Garfish and Barramundi

Seafood

Serves 4

Garfish, Fried or Baked

God in his wisdom, says Giuseppe, has positioned a hole underneath the garfish to make it easier to clean. Insert a sharp knife into the hole, and slit along. Open out, and remove the guts, scraping off any dark film. Then wash the fish under a running tap, and dry.

Brother and sister differ, however, on what happens next. Palmina prefers garfish delicately fried, Giuseppe thinks they are less trouble and taste better baked. The wise person tries both, and refuses to choose without second helpings.

Garfish Palmina-style (Fried)

INGREDIENTS
8 garfish
1 cup of plain flour
lemon slices, to garnish
1 cup of oil (for frying)
salt

Roll each fish in flour. Heat the oil in a frypan large enough to hold four fish (say, about 28 cm). Put in four fish, sprinkling a little salt. After five minutes, turn the heat down, and cook for another eight minutes or until the underside turns golden brown. Using a pair of tongs, turn the fish over and cook the other side in the same way. Take the fish out carefully, and keep warm. Then remove as much as possible of the browned flour-sediment from the oil, reheat the oil and cook the rest of the fish. Serve with lemon slices.

Garfish Giuseppe-style (Baked)

INGREDIENTS
8 garfish
2 tablespoons of oil
50 g of butter
3 lemons
1 teaspoon of salt
1 tablespoon of chopped parsley

Arrange the cleaned garfish in a shallow baking-dish. Cut the lemons in half, and keep one half back for garnish. Squeeze the rest into a bowl, adding two tablespoons of oil, parsley, and some salt, then pour the juice over the garfish. Place butter on top, cover with foil, and leave for fifteen minutes to absorb the flavours.

Bake in a moderate oven for fifteen minutes. Garnish with lemon slices and serve.

Risicato's Sicilian Cookery

Serves 3

Barramundi alla siciliana with Cauliflower Salad

INGREDIENTS
1 large barramundi fillet
(or a comparable pink-and-
white fish with firm flesh)
a pinch of oregano
a twist or two of ground pepper

1 kilo of fresh mussels
3 lemons
2 tablespoons of oil
1½ teaspoons of salt
100 g butter

for the salad
1 cauliflower
parsley

half a cucumber
a dash of wine vinegar

Divide the barramundi fillet into three equal segments, and place in a platter. Squeeze one lemon into a bowl, add olive oil, oregano, salt and pepper. Mix well, and pour over the fish.

Slice the second lemon into thin circles. Put four slices over the central segment of fish, then place the second piece of fish on top, and cover it with slices of lemon. Put the third segment on top of the other two, and cover that also with the remaining slices of lemon. Spoon the surrounding marinade over the fish-deck. Cover the platter with cling-film, and set aside for two hours.

Wash and clean the mussels in plenty of water, removing all grit and fibre from the shells. Put the mussels in a large saucepan, pour in a glass of water (250 ml) and simmer very slowly for about ten to fifteen minutes, until all the shells have opened. It is important to keep the heat low so that the water does not evaporate. Set aside the resulting liquor.

Heat the butter in a frypan large enough to take the three pieces of fish. Lift each piece carefully, and place it in the butter. Keep the heat low. Remove the lemon slices and set them aside for decoration.

Take the flesh out of twelve mussels and set them aside in a bowl. Then strain the marinade off the fish platter and into the bowl.

Cook the fish slowly for five to seven minutes on each side, taking care to lift and turn each piece over carefully. When the fish is nearly done, add the mussels in their marinade to it, so they can warm through. Lift the cooked fish pieces and place them in a large oval platter. The mussel-flesh should be placed, four to each piece, on the fish. Add the juice from the last lemon to the butter sauce in which the fish was cooked, and spoon that over the fish. Arrange the rest of the mussels still in their shells around the fish, alternating with slices of lemon.

The liquor left over after the mussels were cooked should now be poured into sidebowls, sprinkled with parsley, and served as a sauce in which to dip the mussels. The shells themselves make entertaining and remarkably efficient scoops for the broth.

Cauliflower Salad

Trim and wash a whole cauliflower, and place it in a large saucepan with some water. Cover and cook till the cauliflower is done. Let it cool, then carefully separate the florets. Arrange them on a platter, with a large piece at the centre.

Slice the cucumber thinly and use it to decorate. Sprinkle chopped parsley. Then pour two tablespoons of the lemon-and-oil marinade from the fish platter over the cauliflower, and add a dash of good wine-vinegar.

Serves 6

Barramundi in Lemon Butter Sauce

INGREDIENTS
6 barramundi fillets
250 g of butter
juice of 2 lemons
1 clove of garlic, finely chopped
2 tablespoons of oil

salt
pepper
1 tablespoon of chopped parsley
a pinch of oregano

Melt 125 grams of butter in a frypan. Place three barramundi fillets in the melted butter and cook on a low heat for five to seven minutes. Turn over, and cook for another five to seven minutes. Lift the fillets out and keep warm. Melt the rest of the butter and cook the other three fillets in the same way.

Mix in a bowl the oil, lemon juice, garlic, oregano, parsley, a teaspoon of salt and a pinch of pepper. Add to the melted butter in the pan, blend well, and pour over the cooked fillets. Serve warm.

Risicato's Sicilian Cookery

Cozze con fave fresche: Mussels with Broad Beans

Seafood

Serves 6 – 8

Cozze con fave fresche:
Mussels with Broad Beans

INGREDIENTS

1 kilo of fresh mussels	*500 g of frozen broad beans*
(closed and weighty)	*50 g of butter*
2 tablespoons of oil	*2 tablespoons of olive oil*
1 lemon (slice half, squeeze half)	*oregano*
mint leaves	*a few sprigs of parsley*
salt	*(or leaves of lettuce)*

Wash and clean the mussels, removing any grit and fibre. Put in a large saucepan with 250 ml of water (keep water to a minimum). Cook slowly on very low heat till the shells open.

Wash the broad beans in a colander. Cook them in a separate saucepan. If small, they can be cooked slowly in a cup of salted water; if large, boil them in plenty of salted water for about ten minutes. Drain, and return them to their saucepan. Add butter, oil, oregano, fresh mint leaves, and the juice of half a lemon. Adjust the salt, and mix well.

Arrange the broad beans and mussels on a large platter. Decorate with lemon slices and parsley (or lettuce). Mix two tablespoons of olive oil to a cup of broth from the mussels, and spoon the mixture over the beans and mussels. Serve with warm bread.

Serves 4 – 6 for a first course

Fried Sardines

INGREDIENTS

½ kilo of fresh sardines	*1 cup of flour*
oil for frying	*salt*
For the dressing	
juice of a lemon	*1 teaspoon of chopped garlic*
3–4 tablespoons of olive oil	*oregano*
chopped parsley	*salt and pepper*

The sardines should be firm and silvery bright. Cut off the heads, slit the underside to remove the guts, wash and dry thoroughly. Roll them in flour, pressing well in, but shaking off any excess. Heat four tablespoons of oil in a frypan. Put in four sardines, sprinkling a little salt, and fry over a medium heat for seven to ten minutes, using a pair of tongs to turn them. When they are golden, remove, and repeat for the rest. Mix all the ingredients for the dressing, pour it over the sardines, and serve.

Serves 4 – 6

Pesce Spada:
Baked Swordfish with Crisped Potatoes and Celery

Swordfish may not have the dramatic rosy hue of salmon, though its flesh has a subtle visual appeal of its own: pale pink with the occasional barely perceptible purple vein. Its flavour too is subtle and its texture delicate; so that some would say swordfish is more of a treat than salmon. Certainly, swordfish fillets make a fine alternative for that special occasion when guests are ready to try something out of the ordinary.

INGREDIENTS
3 large swordfish fillets
1 lemon
4–5 cloves of garlic, sliced
1 cup of chopped parsley
3 tablespoons of oil

75 g of butter
4 potatoes
5 sticks of celery, tender parts, sliced
a few sprigs of mint
salt and pepper

Melt butter in a saucepan with a little salt and pepper. Place the fish fillets in a baking-tin, and coat both sides of the fillets with melted butter and the juice of half a lemon. Put in a hot oven and bake for fifteen minutes, after which the fillets should be tested to make sure they are cooked through. Strain the juices from the pan, and reserve them. Keep the fish warm.

Peel the potatoes and cut them into small cubes. Sprinkle salt, to taste. Heat oil in a frypan, put in the garlic slices, and fry them lightly. Remove the garlic with a slotted spoon and set aside. Put the potato-cubes into the same pan, adding some chopped parsley and some shredded mint. Stir-fry over a medium heat for about fifteen minutes, until the potatoes are cooked through and have turned crisp on the outside. Put your garlic-slices back, along with the sliced celery, more of the parsley, and half the butter-and-fish juices. Stir well.

Add juice of half a lemon to the butter-and-fish juice, with the remainder of the parsley.

Arrange the fish fillets on a serving-dish, pour the juice over, surround with crisped potatoes, and serve.

POULTRY

Vizzini Streetscape

and GAME

Serves 6 – 8

Pollo agrodolce con sambuca:
Chicken Sambuca

Sambuca *is an anise-flavoured clear liqueur, popular throughout Italy. It is normally drunk with coffee, and for luck three coffee-beans are floated in the top of the glass. But this chicken dish has such a delicate yet tangy flavour, it is well worth the sacrifice of a glass of* sambuca.

INGREDIENTS
- **1½ kilos of chicken drumsticks**, skinned and chopped in half
- **4 large onions**, peeled, sliced thin
- **2 red peppers** (or *1 red, 1 yellow*)
- **4 potatoes**, peeled and quartered
- **salt**
- **1 glass of sambuca**
- **juice of 2 lemons**
- **5 tablespoons of oil**
- **75 g of butter**
- **4 tablespoons of sugar**
- **pepper**

Cut the peppers, taking out their seeds and pith. Slice them into rectangular segments (about 5 x 3 cm). Set aside.

Put the sliced onions into a frypan, and add three tablespoons of oil and a teaspoon of salt. Cover and cook on a very low heat until the onions soften. They should stay white, so keep the heat low.

In another frypan put the pepper segments, adding two tablespoons of oil and one teaspoon of salt. Cover and cook slowly till they soften, being careful not to let them go brown. Take the onions and the peppers out of their respective pans, and set both aside.

Add the butter to the pan in which you fried the onions, and when the butter melts, put in the chicken pieces. Sprinkle a little salt and pepper, then cover and cook slowly, turning them now and then.

Place the potatoes in the frypan in which the peppers were cooked. Add a teaspoon of salt, cover and cook slowly for half an hour, turning them now and then to make sure they do not stick to the pan. They should be golden brown on the outside but still soft within.

When the chicken pieces are cooked through, add the sugar and lemon-juice. Stir well for five minutes, then add your *sambuca*. Cover and cook for another ten minutes.

Arrange the chicken on a platter. Mix in the onions, peppers and potatoes. Pour over it the juices from the pan and serve warm, with crusty bread.

Poultry and Game

Serves 6 – 8

Two-in-One:

Spaghetti in bianco, Pollo alla siciliana:
White Spaghetti and Chicken Siciliana

INGREDIENTS
8 pieces of chicken Maryland
(these should be washed and cleaned, with any excess fat and skin cut off)
3 onions, *sliced*
3 sticks of tender celery *cut into 2 cm pieces*
2 carrots *cut into 2 cm pieces*
10 potatoes, *peeled and halved*
4 fresh tomatoes, *quartered*
2 tablespoons of oil
200 g of grated pecorino
2–3 glasses of white wine
1 litre of hot water
2 teaspoons of salt
half a twist of pepper

Spaghetti in bianco
Cook enough spaghetti for six people (say about five hundred grams), and serve it as first course with the juice of the Chicken Siciliana (but without the vegetables), and sprinkled with some chopped parsley and grated cheese.

Chicken Siciliana
Place the cleaned chicken pieces in a large rectangular oven-dish. Scatter onion slices over them. Drizzle two tablespoons of oil, sprinkle with salt and pepper, mix well, and place in a hot oven. After twenty minutes, take the dish out, turn chicken pieces and onion slices over, and return them to the oven for another twenty minutes. In the meantime, prepare the vegetables.

Take the dish out again, add celery, tomatoes, carrot chunks, potatoes, wine, hot water, and half of the grated pecorino. Add a little more salt to the potatoes, if desired. Cover the whole in foil, and place in the oven to cook for one and a half hours until the chicken is tender and the vegetables cooked. Take the foil away, add the remainder of the pecorino, and return to the oven for a further ten minutes, to allow the potatoes to brown.

Quail, Calamari and Zucchini

Poultry and Game

Serves 4 – 6

Quail

INGREDIENTS
6 quails
1 large onion, *chopped*
1 tablespoon of oil
2 tablespoons of grated pecorino

for the marinade
3 tablespoons of olive oil
juice of 2 lemons
1½ teaspoons of salt
1 teaspoon of pepper

Mix the marinade ingredients in a bowl. Cut each quail along the breastbone, opening it out, then wash and clean thoroughly. Pat them dry.

Heat one tablespoon of oil in a frypan, and cook the chopped onion to a pulp on a very low heat. Mix in the pecorino, and set aside.

Spread out the quails in a baking-dish or in cast-iron platters. Drizzle one tablespoon of the marinade and a little of the onion oil over each quail. Set aside for fifteen minutes.

Turn your oven up to very hot. Put in the quail-tray and bake for twenty minutes on each side, or until they are done. Take out the quails, put a little of your onion-mix in each, and serve.

Serves 6 – 8

Galletto Arrosto: Roast Spatchcock

INGREDIENTS
6 spatchcocks
6 tablespoons of oil
3 lemons
salt

1 teaspoon of ground black pepper
a pinch of oregano (optional)
2 crushed cloves of garlic (optional)

Wash the spatchcocks thoroughly in cold water. Cut off the parson's nose, loose skin and fat. Using a sharp knife, slit each bird along its breastbone, open it out and press flat.

Mix lemon juice, oil, salt, pepper (and the other seasonings, if required) in a bowl. Pour the mixture over the spatchcocks, brushing it well into both sides.

Put into a roasting-pan and roast in a hot oven for twenty minutes. Reduce the heat to medium and cook for a further ten minutes. Then turn the birds over and roast for another half an hour at the same temperature. Finish by turning the heat right down to low and cooking for seven to ten minutes more.

Serves 4

Galletto con Cinzano:
Spatchcock with Cinzano

INGREDIENTS
3 spatchcocks
4 potatoes, sliced 2 cm thick
4 onions, sliced
100 g of butter
salt and pepper
1 large glass of Cinzano Bianco
sprigs of basil

Soak spatchcocks in plenty of cold water. Split in half, then dry thoroughly. Melt butter in a frypan, put in three pieces of spatchcock and brown on a medium heat, turning them over now and then. Cook for ten minutes. Remove, cook the other three pieces, set aside.

Add the sliced onions to the pan, cover and turn down the heat. Cook slowly until the onions start to soften a little, say for about five minutes.

Arrange spatchcocks, onions and sliced potatoes in a baking-dish. Spoon over butter-juices from the pan. Sprinkle salt and a dash of pepper, scatter basil sprigs. Pour *Cinzano* over, cover with foil, put in a medium hot oven, and bake for seventy-five minutes.

Poultry and Game

Serves 4

Champagne Duck

INGREDIENTS
1 large duck (size 18)
6 oranges
1 glass of orange brandy (optional)
salt

1 bottle of champagne
6 teaspoons of sugar
6 potatoes,
peeled and sliced 2 cm thick

accompaniments
5 onions, preferably white
2–3 pieces of tender celery, sliced
a few sprigs of mint

100 g of butter
1 cup of chopped parsley

Wash the duck thoroughly. Remove excess fat. Place in a large saucepan, pour champagne over it and sprinkle a little salt. Simmer for half an hour, turning the duck over carefully at intervals. When the liquid is reduced by half, remove the duck and place in a roasting-tin. Keep the champagne-stock.

Squeeze four oranges and pour the juice over the duck, together with four ladles of champagne-stock. Add orange brandy (if required), and sprinkle sugar. Cover the pan with foil and place in a hot oven. After ten minutes, turn the heat down to medium.

Peel and slice your onions, and put them in a frypan with butter. Cover and cook on a low heat for ten minutes, stirring now and ten, until the onions soften. Don't let them brown.

Arrange potato-slices in an oven-tray, season with a little salt, and pour over the butter-juice from your onion-pan. Place on the top rung of the oven and cook for an hour.

Transfer the cooked onions to a serving-dish. Mix in some chopped parsley, sliced celery, and some shredded mint. Add a little orange brandy (if required), or a little sugar.

After an hour, test the duck by inserting a skewer at a joint. If the juices flow clear and not red, it is done. Remove to a serving platter, and decorate with sliced oranges. Pour the gravy into a gravy-bowl, and serve the duck with potatoes and onions.

Sautéed zucchini make a good accompaniment.

Note
This recipe also works well if you substitute a large, free-range chicken in place of the duck. It has to be a free-range bird, not just on moral grounds, but because the flesh needs to be firmer than that usually found in battery-raised fowls.

Serves 6

Palmina's Chicken Cutlets

INGREDIENTS
500 g (12 fillets) of chicken tenderloin*   *1 clove of garlic*, finely sliced
½ cup of grated pecorino   *2 tablespoons of chopped parsley*
2 cups of crunchy breadcrumbs   *2 eggs*
1 cup of oil (enough for shallow frying)   *salt and pepper*

For the dressing
juice of a lemon   *basil leaves*, shredded
1 clove of garlic, chopped   *salt and pepper*
a pinch of oregano

Sieve breadcrumbs on to a tray. Mix in half a teaspoon of salt, a little pepper, and the sliced garlic and parsley.

Trim the tenderloin fillets, discarding fat and gristle, but keeping any fragments of chicken. Place each fillet on a chopping-board, and press flat with thumb and fingertips. Put the flattened fillets on one half of a dry tea-towel, fold the towel over, and pat dry.

Beat the eggs well. Soak the fillets, four at a time, in the egg. Lift them a piece at a time and place on breadcrumbs. Press the crumbs in, flattening each fillet as you press, so as to expand it to double its original size.

Heat oil in a frypan. Turn the heat down to between medium and low. Place four cutlets in the oil, and let them cook slowly for five minutes on each side. Don't let them brown but adjust your heat so as to get an even, golden colour. Before you fry the next batch, remove any browned crumbs from the frypan with a slotted spoon. Keep the fillets warm.

You may dip any trimmed fragments of chicken in the leftover egg and fry them, so as to get some golden nuggets.

Mix all the ingredients for the dressing in a serving-bowl. Guests can be left to spoon the dressing over their cutlets. A simple tomato, cucumber and basil salad or a green beans salad with mushrooms (see page 102) makes a good accompaniment.

***Note**
It is possible to make veal cutlets by following this recipe, using six veal fillets.

MEAT

Ancestral Stones

Serves 6 – 8

Spezzatino: Sicilian Stew

Spezzatino is a simple winter stew. Traditionally, it is made with beef, but the meat needs to be tender. For better results, you may substitute veal shanks, or a combination of veal shanks and quality beef. The stew may be served with rice, to which you can add some juice from the stew so as to make risotto. For **Spezzatino Bianco***, omit tomatoes, add two cups of water and more wine.*

INGREDIENTS
1 kilo of chuck steak, diced
2 large onions, chopped
3 tablespoons of oil
1 carrot, scraped and diced
½ kilo of peas
6 potatoes, peeled and quartered
salt

or **4 veal shanks**
2 tablespoons of chopped garlic
800 g of tinned tomatoes
2 sticks of celery, diced
1 medium glass of white wine
3 tablespoons of grated pecorino
pepper

Heat the oil in a large saucepan. Add onions and garlic, and soften on a low heat. Add the diced beef, with two teaspoons of salt, and pepper. Stir well. Cook for ten minutes.

Add the tomatoes, diced carrots and celery. A little more salt can be added now, if required. Stir, and pour the wine in. Cook for another fifteen minutes, then add the peas and potatoes. Cook for an hour or so, until the beef is done.

Serves 6 – 8

Spezzatino di pollo: Chicken Stew

This can be made from left-over chicken after you have prepared chicken soup (page 17).

INGREDIENTS
chicken meat (from 2 thighs and legs)
250 g of frozen peas
2–3 tablespoons of chopped parsley
200 g of tomatoes

2 large onions, sliced
3 tablespoons of oil
4 potatoes, peeled, sliced 2 cm thick
salt and pepper

Cut cooked chicken into large chunks. Put the peas in a bowl, cover with cold water for ten minutes. Heat oil in a frypan, add the onions and peas, and cook slowly for ten minutes.

Pour one litre of water into a saucepan. Add the cut-up chicken, peas and tomatoes, with the chopped parsley, and finally put in the potatoes, with a teaspoon of salt. Cover, and cook slowly for about thirty to forty minutes.

Meat

Serves 6 – 8

Vitello al forno alla Zilla Risicato:
Signora Risicato's Roast Veal

This recipe is dedicated in loving memory to a gracious and cultivated Australian lady who took a wandering Sicilian, his people, and his home town of Vizzini to her heart, and among her many talents learned to cook this Sicilian dish even better than the people of the place.

INGREDIENTS
1½ kilos of roasting veal, preferably boneless (if on the bone, 2 kilos)
6 large cloves of garlic, sliced
1 glass of white wine
6 potatoes, peeled and cut into thick slices
1 lemon
4 tablespoons of oil
25 g of butter
1 glass of whisky (optional)
sprigs of rosemary
salt and pepper

Wash the veal and place it in a roasting-tin. With a sharp knife, make incisions on the surface of the meat and insert cloves of garlic and some of the rosemary.

Sprinkle on the meat two teaspoons of salt and one teaspoon of ground pepper (or more, depending on your taste), and rub them in well. Pour oil and wine, and smear them over thoroughly. Cover and leave for at least half an hour.

Heat the oven to very hot. Put in your veal in its roasting-tin, and turn the setting down to low. After fifteen minutes, take out and baste the meat thoroughly. Return the veal to the oven for a further fifteen minutes. Take it out again, add the potatoes with more sprigs of rosemary, cover the tin with foil, and cook on a low heat for one hour.

Take the roast from the oven, pour a glass of whisky over, spread butter on it, and return to the oven, still covered, for another fifteen minutes. When the meat is ready, take off its foil, squeeze a lemon over it and (if no whisky has been used) sprinkle a little sugar. Let it stand for ten minutes before carving. Serve with the potatoes and a salad.

Note
The juice from this roast is exquisite and will make a superb *Spaghetti in bianco* for a first course. Simply pour the juice over some cooked spaghetti, stirring in some grated pecorino and fresh basil.

Serves 6

Vitello rosa:
Pink Veal

INGREDIENTS
600 g of veal fillets
2 onions, sliced
1 tablespoon of chopped garlic
2 tablespoons of chopped parsley
3 tablespoons of Napoletana sauce
salt and pepper
4 potatoes, peeled and cut into slices 1 cm thick
2 tablespoons of oil
½ glass of white wine
2 tablespoons of grated pecorino

Cut the veal fillets into strips two centimetres wide. Heat one tablespoon of oil in a frypan, and place the veal strips in it, with one teaspoon of salt and a pinch of pepper. Cook on a medium heat, giving five minutes to each side. Add a little of the parsley, the garlic and half the wine, and cook for another five minutes. Remove both veal and juices from the pan and set them aside.

Put the onions in the pan, together with one tablespoon of oil and half a teaspoon of salt, and brown them lightly over a medium heat. Pour in the rest of the wine, and sprinkle a little more of the parsley. Return the veal strips and their juices to the pan, adding three tablespoons of Napoletana sauce (see page 21). Add some water and cook slowly for twenty minutes.

Arrange the sliced potatoes over the veal, cover the pan, and cook for another forty minutes, till the potatoes are properly done. Just before you serve, sprinkle over the veal some cheese and the remaining parsley.

Serves 6

Vitello bianco:
White Veal

INGREDIENTS: **as above**, substituting for Napoletana sauce
½ glass of marsala or *white wine*

Proceed as for *Vitello rosa* above. However, when you have returned the veal strips with their juices to the pan, omit the Napoletana sauce and add in its place half a glass of marsala or another half-glass of white wine.

Meat

Makes 18

Polpette alla Palmina:
Palmina's Meat-Patties

INGREDIENTS
125 g of minced veal
4 tablespoons of grated pecorino
6–8 tablespoons of oil
salt

2 eggs
2 tablespoons of chopped parsley
½ glass of white wine

Put minced veal in a bowl, and break eggs into it. Add pecorino, one tablespoon of parsley, one and a half teaspoons of salt, and mix well. Cover and refrigerate for an hour.

Pour the wine into a saucer, and moisten your fingers and palms with it. Take a spoonful of the meat and shape into a patty, dipping your fingers in wine so as to get a smooth finish. Repeat, till the meat is used up.

Heat the oil in a frypan. When the oil gets very hot, put in the patties, about six or eight at a time. Turn the heat down a little, and let the patties cook for five minutes. Ease them with a flat spatula, turn them over, and cook for another five minutes. Repeat the process till the patties are cooked through: they should be golden brown outside but white inside.

Lift the patties out and arrange in a plate. Sprinkle with chopped parsley and serve hot.

Serves 4 – 6

Dolcissimi fegatini di pollo:
Sweet Chicken Livers

INGREDIENTS
500 g of chicken livers
3 tablespoons of oil
salt

3 white onions, sliced
2 tablespoons of wine vinegar
pepper

Wash the livers and remove any gristle. Heat oil in a frypan, put in the sliced onions with one teaspoon of salt and some pepper. Cook on a medium heat for ten minutes, then add the livers, turn the heat down, and cook for another fifteen minutes. Add your wine vinegar, cover, and cook on a very low heat for fifeen minutes more. When the liver is no longer red, it is ready to serve.

Risicato's Sicilian Cookery

Maiale ripieno e peperoni ripieni:
Stuffed Pork and Capsicums

Meat

Serves 4

Mama Risicato's Maiale ripieno:
Stuffed Pork Steaks with Mushroom Risotto

For this scrumptious dish you will need thick pork chops. Get the butcher to slit the pork chops into butterfly-shapes. Trim their edges to make a neat curve. The trimmed bits can later be used, without their fat, in the mushroom risotto that accompanies this dish.

INGREDIENTS
4 pork butterfly-steaks	**2 onions**, *finely chopped*
10 stoned olives, *chopped*	**125 g button mushrooms**, *chopped*
6–8 tablespoons of oil	**1 cup of chopped parsley**
1 glass of red wine	**1 cup of grated pecorino**
400 g of tinned tomatoes	**3 cloves of garlic**, *chopped*
200 g of uncooked rice	**salt**
pepper	**strong toothpicks**

Make Napoletana sauce with four hundred grams of tomatoes, chopped garlic and one tablespoon of oil (see page 21).

Spread flat the butterfly-steaks and beat them gently with a mallet. Fold over, and beat a little more.

Put the chopped onions into a frypan, with one teaspoon of salt, pepper, and three tablespoons of oil. Cook slowly with a lid on for ten minutes, until the onions soften. Add fine-chopped mushrooms and cook for another five minutes. Add half the pecorino, a little at a time. Add the olives, and cook for five minutes more. Mix in half the parsley, take out and set aside.

Rinse the frypan, dry it, and put in three tablespoons of oil. Turn the heat up, place the butterfly-steaks in the pan one at a time, spreading them out, and fry on each side. Hold each steak down flat as it fries, taking care not to break the joint; this will prevent it from curling up.

Take the steaks out and keep the juices. Once the meat is cool enough to handle, spread each steak out and put the stuffing on one half: the stuffing is three tablespoons of the mushroom-mix, with a little parsley and a tablespoon of Napoletana sauce. Sprinkle a little pecorino over the whole, then fold over and secure the edges of the steak with

(see over)

two or three toothpicks. Place the stuffed steaks in a baking-dish. Then pour over the juices from the frypan, add the red wine, cover the dish with foil, seal well, and bake in a medium-hot oven for one hour.

Mushroom Risotto
Cook the rice in plenty of water. Drain it, rinse, and cool. Fry the trimmed ends of pork in a frypan with a little oil, mix in the leftover stuffing with three tablespoons of Napoletana sauce, a little pecorino and some chopped parsley.

When the steaks are ready, serve with the risotto and any spare Napoletana sauce.

Serves 4

Costate di maiale ripiene:
Stuffed Pork Chops

INGREDIENTS
4 boneless pork chops (2 cm thick)
1 lemon
4–5 firm, white, large mushrooms
(optional)
3 tablespoons of grated pecorino
25 g of butter

1 cup of flour
1 onion, finely chopped
1 cup of chopped parsley
3 tablespoons of cooked rice
4 tablespoons of oil
salt

Wash the pork chops, then dry them in a towel. Using a sharp knife, make a slit no more than two centimetres long in the side of each chop opposite to the rind. Move the knife horizontally inside the chop to create a pocket, but take care not to pierce the rind or break through the sides of the chop at any point. Spread some flour on a plate and dust each chop thoroughly with it.

Heat two tablespoons of oil in a frypan. Put in your chopped onion with half a teaspoon of salt, and cook slowly for five minutes until the onion softens. Add half the parsley, a squeeze of lemon-juice, and two tablespoons of grated pecorino.

Take the pan off the heat, and mix in three tablespoons of cooked rice. Cool a little longer, then mix in one more tablespoon of pecorino. Divide the mix into four portions and carefully stuff each chop, closing the opening with two toothpicks. Dust the chops again with flour.

Meat

In a large frypan, melt the butter in two tablespoons of oil, adding a pinch of salt. Put in the chops, turn the heat down to low, cover and cook for five minutes. Then turn the chops over, cover again, and cook for thirty minutes or more. It is essential to cook pork thoroughly, so test to make sure they are done through.

Peel and slice each mushroom across to make two disks (see the instructions on page 89). Squeeze a little more lemon-juice into the frypan, place the mushroom-disks in it, sprinkle some parsley, and cook until tender.

Serve the pork chops topped with mushrooms, chopped parsley, and slices of lemon. A plain green salad of lettuce, cucumber, black olives, fresh parsley and basil makes a refreshing accompaniment.

Serves 3

Ossobuco:

Baked Knuckles of Veal

INGREDIENTS
6 pieces of veal on the knuckle
½ cup of plain flour
4 tablespoons of oil
basil leaves
400 g of tomatoes
a glass of white wine (optional)
2 cloves of garlic, sliced
salt and pepper

Spread flour on a plate. Press the veal pieces well in, so as to coat thoroughly. Heat oil in a frypan, adding one teaspoon of salt. Brown the veal pieces on a medium heat, turning them over after five minutes. Then lower the heat, cover, and cook for twenty minutes. Transfer to a baking-dish.

Cook garlic and tomatoes, with a pinch of salt and pepper and some basil, for five minutes. Pour the mix over the veal, add your white wine, cover, and bake in a medium hot oven for one hour.

72 *Ernesto Ventura (Giovanni Piluso) as Arturo in 'I Puritani'*

Bistecca Bellini

Serves 4 – 6

Vincenzo Bellini (1801 – 1835) is a favourite son of Catania, the nearest large town in Sicily to Vizzini. The grace and charm of Bellini's personality was reflected in the lyricism of the operas he created before his tragically early death in Paris, and it is also represented in this delicate dish that Giuseppe has created to honour him. Together with Bellini, Giuseppe dedicates his Bistecca Bellini *to his friend, the tenor Ernesto Ventura, who was born Giovanni Piluso in Vizzini, and is seen opposite in Giuseppe's portrait of him as Arturo in Bellini's* I Puritani. *In the background is the opera house of Catania, where Ernesto Ventura sang the major tenor role in Bellini's last and greatest opera.*

INGREDIENTS
- **3 large sirloin steaks (1400 g)**
- **2 onions**, finely chopped
- **2 red capsicums** (or **1 red, 1 yellow**)
- **1 anchovy fillet**
- **fresh basil**
- **salt and pepper**
- **50 g of butter** or **margarine**
- **1 tablespoon of chopped garlic**
- **2 tablespoons of tuna**
- **2 tablespoons of chopped parsley**
- **1 tablespoon of olive oil**

Roast the capsicums on a gas-ring or in the oven (see page 98). Cool them, peel, and discard pith and seeds. Cut into strips, and spoon over them one tablespoon of olive oil, one teaspoon of chopped garlic, and a little salt and pepper. Set aside.

Trim and cut the steak into serving portions. Heat a frypan, then take it off the heat, place butter in it, and let the butter melt. Add one teaspoon of salt.

Put chopped onions and the rest of the garlic in another frypan. Spoon half the melted butter over the onions. Put the onion-pan on a medium heat, and cook slowly till the onions become mushy, say for ten minutes. Chop your tuna and anchovy and add to the onions, along with the parsley. Mix well, and cook for three minutes.

Place your first frypan with the melted butter on the stove. Turn up the heat, and put in the steak pieces, three at a time. Turn down the heat to medium and cook for seven minutes, before turning over for a further seven minutes. Spoon half the onion-and-tuna mix over the meat, and cook till the steaks are done. Lift out and keep warm. Repeat the process with the three remaining steaks.

Arrange the steaks on a serving-platter. Decorate each steak with strips of roasted capsicum and basil leaves. Spoon the pan-juices over each. A refreshing side-dish is plain boiled endive to which a tablespoon of olive oil has been added.

Risicato's Sicilian Cookery

Giovanni Verga

Meat

Serves 6 – 8

Coniglio Verga:
Rabbit Verga

Vizzini is famous as the home of the great novelist Giovanni Verga (1840–1922). When in his early twenties, Verga met in Milan a fellow-Sicilian from the neighbouring town of Mineo, Luigi Capuana, who introduced him to Zola and the French school of naturalism. Though influenced by 'realist' theory, Verga was primarily a good storyteller whose recurrent theme was the struggle of life, especially for those in humble circumstances.

He retained an affection for the food of his own people, sharing a passion for rabbit with the composer Piero Mascagni, who used a Verga story for his opera Cavalleria Rusticana *(set in Vizzini). Oddly, Mascagni omitted to get Verga's permission beforehand, perhaps presuming on their friendship; the matter had to be sorted out afterwards, perhaps over this very dish. The two friends would meet regularly in Vizzini for the hunting season, with the particular intention of eating rabbit together, cooked in the traditional way.*

INGREDIENTS
2 rabbits
4 cloves of garlic, chopped
flour for coating
2 cups of white vinegar
1 tablespoon of capers
1 stick of celery, chopped
salt

2 onions, sliced
chopped parsley
oil
1 glass of wine
400 g of tomatoes
some green olives
pepper

Get your butcher to cut the rabbit into chunks. Soak them overnight in plenty of water (about 3 litres), with the vinegar. Dry the pieces and coat them with flour.

Heat four tablespoons of oil in a frypan, put in a few pieces of meat at a time, and cook until they turn golden. Transfer the meat to a large saucepan.

Add a little more oil to the frypan if needed and toss in the chopped garlic, parsley and onions. Add two teaspoons of salt, and cook slowly for ten minutes until the onions soften. Then add them to the meat in the saucepan. Stir the contents over a low heat for ten to fifteen minutes.

Pour in a glass of white wine, add the tomatoes, chopped celery, and pepper. Transfer the contents to a baking-dish, stir in capers and olives, cover with foil, and cook in a moderate oven for about an hour and a quarter. Serve with roast potatoes and vegetables, as required.

Serves 6 – 8

Capretto Vermouth:
Milk-fed Goat (or Young Lamb) with Vermouth

Milk-fed goat (which we were once able to call 'kid', though that word might now have alarming implications in a recipe) has equal popularity in Sicily with agnello, *young lamb. This simple yet sweet-tasting roast can be made with either milk-fed goat on the bone or with roasting pieces of spring lamb.*

> INGREDIENTS
> **2 large pieces of milk-fed goat on the bone**
> or **roasting pieces of lamb**
> **2 glasses of vermouth**
> **2 tablespoons of oil**
> **6 potatoes**, peeled and quartered
> **500 g of peas**
> **salt**
> **pepper**

Put the meat in a roasting-pan, and rub it over with salt and pepper. Coat with oil, and pour your vermouth over it. Bake in a hot oven for twenty minutes, turn the meat over, baste it, and bake for ten minutes more. Then turn down the heat to medium. Cover the dish with foil, and after another half an hour, put in the potatoes.

Pour some hot water over the peas, drain them and add them to the contents of the roasting-pan. Cover, and bake for another hour. Test if the meat and potatoes are done, and cook them longer if necessary.

Serve with the juices from the pan.

Note
Since baby goat is traditional fare at Easter, two more recipes can be found under *'Festival Fare'* (pages 81 and 83). These recipes also taste just as good with young spring lamb.

FARE FOR FESTIVALS

A Banquet for Vizzini

EASTER DAY
and the
FEAST OF SAN GREGORIO

Mandalion

Festival Fare

The Easter Festival

'A Man of Sorrows'

Throughout Good Friday, it is traditional for the people of Vizzini to fast. But in the week before Easter, preparations for the feast of Christ's Resurrection are well advanced. Young kids, milk-fed goats, are as traditional fare at Easter as is the turkey at Christmas in Anglo-Saxon cultures. In Giuseppe's youth, vendors would come into the market with young goats and haggle with prospective buyers. Once a price was agreed, the vendor would cut the goat's throat in front of the customer. Giuseppe rather hopes this custom has been discontinued; but not the habit of preparing a variety of Easter fare from ricotta cheese (see our section on 'Versatile Ricotta').

Easter Day is marked by special celebrations in the town square of Vizzini. The statues of San Giovanni Evangelista and the Virgin Mary, both dressed in black, are brought out and come into the square from opposite sides.

San Giovanni Evangelista goes to greet the Virgin with the joyful news of Christ's resurrection. She shakes her head, not quite believing what San Giovanni Evangelista has told her. San Giovanni Evangelista retreats, but makes a second foray to the centre of the square and once again announces that Christ has arisen. The Virgin still shakes her head.

On the third occasion, Jesus himself is brought forth, and the Virgin comes to meet him halfway. Great rejoicing ensues, fireworks burst in the sky overhead, and the crowd embrace one another in joy, crying out 'The Lord has arisen!'

On Easter afternoon, a stage is erected in the town square, and people bring bread, cheese, eggs and other farm produce for a public auction. Money raised by the auction goes to church charities.

CAPRETTO AL FORNO

Festival Fare

Serves 6 – 8

Capretto al forno coi funghi:
Milk-fed Goat with Mushrooms

INGREDIENTS
2 legs and shanks of milk-fed goat
8 onions, peeled and cut in halves
½ kilo of button mushrooms
6 tablespoons of oil
8 potatoes, peeled and cut in halves
salt and pepper
2 lemons
125 g of butter
4 glasses of white wine
3 cloves of chopped garlic
3 tablespoons of sugar

Mix oil, the juice of two lemons, three teaspoons of salt and some pepper in a bowl so as to make a marinade.

Wash and pat dry your joints of meat. Brush each piece generously with marinade, then put them in a roasting-pan. Pour on two glasses of white wine.

Place the pan in a medium hot oven and bake uncovered for fifteen minutes. (Meanwhile, dip your onion-halves in marinade, and wash and dry the mushrooms.)

Take out the pan and turn the meat over, then continue baking for another fifteen minutes. Then add 125 grams of butter and the rest of the wine. Turn the meat over once more and bake uncovered for another ten minutes.

Take the pan out again and add your potatoes and onions. Baste them well with the pan-juices, then cover with foil, sealing it carefully, and return to the oven. Turn down to a low heat, and bake for half an hour.

Add three tablespoons of sugar to the leftover marinade, undo the foil, and baste the potatoes once more with pan-juices and the marinade. Re-arrange the foil and return the pan to the oven for a further half an hour, till the potatoes are properly cooked.

Take the meat out, put your mushrooms in the pan, and cook in the oven for ten minutes.

Arrange the meat on a platter, with potatoes and mushrooms around it.

Capretto alla siciliana: Milk-Fed Goat

Festival Fare

Serves 6 – 8

Capretto alla siciliana:
Milk-fed Goat

Get the butcher to cut the capretto *into four portions. One portion can be cut into eight or ten chunks.*

> INGREDIENTS
> **8–10 chunks of milk-fed goat**
> **8 onions**, *sliced*
> **1 kilo of fresh tomatoes**, *scalded, peeled and chopped*
> **125 g of butter**
> **2–3 glasses of white wine**
> **8 tablespoons of oil**
> **3 cloves of chopped garlic**
> **4 potatoes**, *peeled and sliced thick (2 cm)*
> **1 tablespoon of oregano**
> **a dash of liqueur** *(optional)*
> **salt**

The night before cooking, wash and pat dry the meat chunks. Sprinkle three teaspoons of salt and some twists of pepper, rubbing well in. Cover and leave in the fridge.

Before cooking, drain off any excess water. Heat four tablespoons of oil in a deep frypan. Put in half the sliced onions and the meat chunks, and cook over a medium heat for about twenty minutes, turning now and then. Add ninety grams of butter.

In another frypan fry the rest of the onions in two tablespoons of oil till they are golden, and then pour the lot over the meat. Add two or three glasses of white wine, and let the wine evaporate for ten minutes.

Heat another tablespoon of oil in the onion pan, put in the chopped garlic, and when it softens add the chopped tomatoes and cook for five minutes.

Transfer all ingredients to an oblong baking-dish. Add a dash of liqueur, if required. Cover with potato pieces, spreading the remainder of the butter over the potatoes as it melts. Sprinkle a tablespoon of oregano, then cover with foil, and bake in a medium hot oven for forty-five minutes.

Risicato's Sicilian Cookery

*A New Image of San Gregorio
Carried in Procession through Vizzini*

Festival Fare

The Feast of San Gregorio

San Gregorio, Pope Gregory the Great (AD 590–604), is patron saint of Vizzini. Though he was born in Rome, Sicilians see him as their own, for he utilized all his inherited wealth to establish six monasteries on his estates in the island. However, he is not carried in procession on his feast day, but only when the town is in special need. At the first sign of an earth tremor, whether it is day or night, the saint is fetched from his church and carried through the streets of Vizzini, for he is believed to be particularly effective against earthquakes.

Alas, not even the images of saints are protected from human wrongdoing. In the year in which Giuseppe was painting scenes of his native town, the statue of San Gregorio was stolen for its gold, stripped and left broken in a ditch. The town ordered a replacement; and on the day when the new image was brought from the railway station and carried through the streets of Vizzini into the church of San Gregorio, Giuseppe caught a rare picture of the saint in joyous procession, bedecked with flowers, and accompanied by the Italian flag and the town band.

Serves 6

Trippa pa Festa do Santo Patrone di Vizzini:
Saint Gregory's Tripe

This is the dish for Saint Gregory's Day; though when asked why, neither Giuseppe nor Palmina were able to say more than it was 'traditional'. Traditional too is the accompaniment of Chicory or Endive Salad *(page 102).*

INGREDIENTS
1 kilo of tripe
1 onion, roughly chopped
200 g of tinned tomatoes
1 cup of chopped parsley
salt and pepper

4 potatoes
1 tablespoon of chopped garlic
½ cup of oil
1 cup of grated pecorino

Make sure the tripe is white. Cut it into strips, and put it in a saucepan of water with a teaspoon of salt. Bring to the boil, then remove from the heat and drain.

Put the chopped onion, garlic, half a teaspoon of salt, and oil into a frypan. Cook slowly for five minutes, then add some chopped parsley and the chopped tomatoes. Mash well for five minutes. Add the drained tripe, a pinch of pepper, and one tablespoon of pecorino. Stir well, and cook on a low heat for fifteen minutes.

Peel and cut the potatoes into thick slices. Arrange them on top of the tripe and add more parsley. Cover and cook for twenty minutes, or until the potatoes are done. Just before serving, sprinkle more parsley and two tablespoons of pecorino.

Risicato's Sicilian Cookery

Scarpia's Private Feast

In Act II of Giacomo Puccini's Tosca, *the villainous head of Rome's secret police, Baron Scarpia, interrupts 'la povera mia cena', his 'simple supper', to entrap the heroine whose beauty 'makes him forget God'. He subjects her lover, Cavaradossi, to torture in her hearing, but offers her safe conduct to freedom for them both if she will submit to Scarpia's desires. But at what he thinks is his moment of triumph, Tosca snatches a knife from his supper-table and plunges it in his breast. We have re-created Scarpia's 'simple' but of course stimulating repast:* brodino, *pigeon-broth (page 17), this* bistecca ai funghi, *and (had he lived to enjoy it) a dessert of peaches in wine (page 111).*

Serves 4

Bistecca ai funghi

Scarpia would have had funghi porcini *with his beefsteak; but these are not easy to find outside Italy. This recipe makes culinary and artistic use of those saucer-sized mushrooms which it seems a pity to chop into fragments. Palmina suggests you take a tape-measure to market, and buy those that are fresh, very firm, and at least ten centimetres across.*

INGREDIENTS
4 Scotch fillets of beef
6 large cloves of garlic,
cut into chunky slices
1 lemon
1 tablespoon of parsley

4 saucer-sized mushrooms
4 tablespoons of oil
25 g of butter
1 tablespoon of chopped mint
salt and pepper

Peel the mushrooms. Holding the stalk in hand, slice carefully across the cap to get two to three disks from each, about half a centimetre thick. Trim and slice the rest, and set aside.

Heat oil and butter in a heavy frypan, then add half a teaspoon of salt. Put in the garlic-slices, and cook on a low heat for five minutes until they turn golden. Remove and set aside. Turn up the heat a little, put in your beef-fillets, then turn the heat to low. Cover and cook for seven minutes before turning the fillets over. Cook for another ten minutes more, then test a ragged end to see if it is done (Scarpia would prefer his medium-rare).

Remove the fillets and keep them warm. Add the juice of a lemon to the pan, more salt, a pinch of pepper, some parsley and mint. Place as many mushroom-disks as can be fitted in the pan. Cover and cook on a low heat for five minutes, turn over carefully and cook for another five. Remove and keep warm. Cook the rest in the same way.

Arrange the beef-fillets in a serving-dish, put a large mushroom-disk on each, top it with a smaller disk, and finish with fried garlic-slices. Sprinkle the remaining parsley and mint, and serve with juices from the pan.

SALADS, BEANS

Taormina

and
VEGETABLES

Salads, Beans and Vegetables

Dried beans are not only highly nutritious, they are also relatively inexpensive. In consequence, Sicilian cooking makes great use of them, not only for soups but also for salads. The beans must always be soaked overnight. If they are cooked slowly and thoroughly, and (in particular) if all the scum is removed as it rises to the surface, they are easily digestible and cause no unpleasant flatulence.

When you cook beans for a soup, you might as well reserve some cooked beans for inclusion in a salad. The salad should have a simple dressing of olive-oil (three parts) and wine vinegar (one part), together with fresh herbs (oregano, parsley and basil). Here are some suggestions for interesting combinations:

Fagioli (borlotti beans): *served with hard-boiled eggs, quartered, and with slivers of red onions* (cipolle-calabresi)*;*
Fave fresche (broad beans): *served with sliced, raw mushrooms;*
Fagioli con la cucuzza: *served according to the recipe on page 13.*

As for visual effect, try a platter of Risotto Risicato *(page 35), surrounded by some bean salads, fringed with leaves from the yellow heart of lettuce or endive, a few slices of fennel-bulb, slivers of cucumber, and some black olives. It looks delightful and tastes delicious.*

Salads, Beans and Vegetables

Serves 6 – 8

Carciofi al cartoccio: Artichokes in Foil

INGREDIENTS
6–8 artichokes
4 tablespoons of olive oil
or *melted butter*
1 lemon
strong aluminium foil

parsley (optional)
breadcrumbs (optional)
grated pecorino (optional)
salt and pepper

Leave five centimetres of stem and cut off the rest. Hold each artichoke upright and take one centimetre from the top. Turn it upside down and give a mild tap to loosen the leaves.

Arrange four artichokes in a generous double layer of foil, sprinkle some salt, pour some oil or melted butter, with a squeeze of lemon-juice. You may also stuff the leaves with a mixture of chopped parsley, breadcrumbs and grated pecorino, pressing a little down between the leaves. Fold the foil over loosely, and twist it at the top to make a parcel.

Place the parcels in a baking-tin and bake in a hot oven for an hour. When you undo the parcels to serve, take care to preserve the juices. No knife and fork are required for eating this dish: it is what Giuseppe calls 'a finger-job'. Don't neglect the stem, for it is as delicious as the heart of the artichoke. The maestro, with years of serving artichokes to the uninitiated behind him, thinks it advisable to remind guests that the leaves should be sucked (or scraped through the teeth) and discarded, and any hairs around the heart of the artichoke ought to be removed.

Serves 4

Mushroom Saucers

INGREDIENTS
4 saucer-sized mushrooms
25 g of butter
chopped parsley

1 lemon
1 tablespoon of oil
salt and pepper

When large, almost saucer-sized mushrooms are available, it seems a pity to chop them up. Choose firm, white, fleshy ones. Peel them, and holding the stalk in your hand, carefully slice across the cap to get two or three disks from each, each about half a centimetre thick. Trim and slice the rest.

Melt butter in oil in a frypan, then add the juice of one lemon, with a pinch of salt and pepper. Put in the mushroom-disks, cover them, and cook slowly for five minutes on each side. Sprinkle with chopped parsley and serve.

Risicato's Sicilian Cookery

Rooftops of Vizzini

Salads, Beans and Vegetables

Serves 6

Melanzane ripiene:
Stuffed Eggplants or Aubergines

INGREDIENTS
4 eggplants
4 cloves of garlic, chopped
1½ tablespoons of oil
1 cup of cooked rice
1 cup of chopped parsley
125 g of grated mozzarella
2 medium size onions, sliced and chopped
200 gm of tuna, drained and chopped
2 tablespoons of grated pecorino
salt

(The recipe allows for two extra eggplant-shells, so guests may have seconds.)

Top and tail the eggplants. Cut them in half lengthwise. Take a slice off the curved part so that the eggplant-shell can sit well in the pan. Scoop out the soft white part from the eggplants, using a spoon. Chop it and put aside.

Place the scooped-out shells in a large saucepan, sprinkle with salt and cover with water.

Heat the oil in a frypan. Put in the onions and garlic, and soften them on a low heat, keeping the pan covered. Add the chopped white part of the eggplant and the chopped tuna, and cook for another ten minutes. Add the cooked rice and chopped parsley. Take it off the heat, add the pecorino and mix well.

Drain the eggplant-shells and dry them thoroughly. Brush a shallow oven-proof pan with oil. Place the eggplant-shells in the pan, and brush with oil. Place in a hot oven for twenty to thirty minutes until the shells are soft.

Take out the pan, and spoon the tuna-rice filling into the eggplant-shells. Return to the oven for another ten minutes. Take out again, top with grated mozzarella, and return to the oven briefly until the cheese melts.

Serve with a mushroom salad.

Note
There are recipes for alternative fillings on pages 97 and 98 under *Stuffed Capiscums and Tomatoes*, and these work equally well if used to stuff eggplant.

Serves 4

Involtini di melanzane:
Eggplant Rolls

INGREDIENTS
2 bundles of asparagus (24 spears)
4 eggs, boiled, peeled and sliced
200 g of Napoletana sauce
salt
2 large eggplants
6 tablespoons of oil
2 tablespoons of grated pecorino
toothpicks

Wash the eggplants. Place them on their side and take a slim slice off lengthwise, top and bottom, so as to remove any hard skin. Then cut each eggplant lengthwise into four thick slices. Sprinkle salt, cover, and set aside for an hour.

Pat them dry on a towel or paper towel. Pour three tablespoons of oil into a bowl, and dip the eggplant slices so as to cover both sides with oil. Place them on the rack of a hot oven, with a tray underneath to catch juices. Roast for fifteen minutes, turn them over, and roast for another fifteen minutes, taking care not to break them. They should be soft enough to roll; but if the edges are too stiff and dry, peel them or snip them off with a pair of kitchen scissors.

Stir-fry the asparagus in three tablespoons of oil. Sprinkle a little pecorino on a slice of eggplant. Place three asparagus spears across, with the tips hanging over one side. Dab some Napoletana sauce. Add two slices of boiled egg, roll, and secure with a toothpick. Repeat the same process for the rest.

Serves 6

Melanzane fritte: Fried Eggplant

INGREDIENTS
2 large, firm eggplants
salt
oil for shallow frying

Peel and slice the eggplants lengthwise into thick (half centimetre) slices. Drop them immediately into a bowl of salted water, and let them soak for an hour. Using a sharp knife lightly, remove excess seeds from the surface, taking care not to break the slice. Dry the slices thoroughly, using a tea-towel. Heat about one centimetre depth of oil in a frypan. Put in two to three slices at a time, and fry over medium heat for about five minutes on each side, until they turn soft inside and pale brown on the outside.

Salads, Beans and Vegetables

Serves 6 – 8

Melanzane alla parmigiana
Layered Eggplant in Tomato Sauce

The name of this dish derives from the parmesan cheese used to flavour layered eggplant. However, in this recipe pecorino is preferred.

It is easy to spoil the look of this popular dish if the eggplants are allowed to get too dry or if tomato paste is used to make the sauce. Sauce made with tomato paste lacks flavour and forms an ugly dried edge. This Sicilian variation takes a little more time and care; but the final result is moist, elegant, and well worth the effort.

> INGREDIENTS
> **4 large eggplants**
> **4 capsicum** (green, red or yellow)
> **360 ml of oil**
> **6 potatoes,** *peeled and sliced thin*
> **3 tablespoons of chopped garlic**
> **800 g of tinned tomatoes**
> **250 g of grated parmesan** or ***percorino* cheese**
> **2–3 tablespoons of chopped parsley**
> **salt**

Each item of this recipe has to be prepared separately and then arranged in layers. For the final cooking, you need a large, deep baking-dish.

Cut the stalks off the eggplants. Slice them lengthwise in one centimetre slices. Discard the dark-skinned end-pieces. Place the rest in a tray, sprinkle salt, cover with a cloth and set aside.

Cut the capsicums across, discarding the pith and seeds. Slice into thin strips.

Pour a cup of oil into a shallow bowl. Dip both sides of each eggplant slice in the oil. Turn your oven to high heat. Arrange the eggplant slices straight on to the oven-racks, and roast them for fifteen minutes. Then turn them over and roast the other side for another fifteen minutes. Roast the slices in batches, if necessary. (It helps to place a baking-dish under the eggplants to catch any juices.)

(see over)

Heat two tablespoons of oil in a frypan. Put in the capsicum-strips and sprinkle salt. Cover and cook slowly, stirring frequently, for about fifteen minutes. Add two tablespoons of garlic. Cover and cook for a further five minutes until the capsicum-strips become soft.

Blanch the sliced potatoes in salted water for three minutes. Drain them, transfer to a greased baking-tray, brush with a little oil, and sprinkle salt. Place on the bottom-rung of the oven. Cook for thirty minutes, or until the potatoes are cooked through.

To prepare tomato sauce
Heat a tablespoon of oil in a saucepan. Add one tablespoon of chopped garlic. Soften the garlic on a low heat. Add tomatoes and salt. Cook slowly for fifteen minutes, mashing the tomatoes with a ladle.

For the final cooking
Coat a deep baking-dish with two tablespoons of the tomato sauce. Place a layer of roasted eggplant, coat with tomato sauce, sprinkle cheese. Place a layer of sliced potatoes. Dab on some sauce, sprinkle some cheese. Cover the potatoes with capsicum-strips, reserving a few capsicum-strips for the uppermost layer. Repeat the process, starting with eggplant slices. Cover the topmost layer of eggplant with capsicum-strips. Cover the dish with aluminium foil and return to the oven. Turn the heat down and cook on low heat for about an hour.

Serves 4 – 6

Crisped Potatoes with Celery

INGREDIENTS
5 potatoes
5 sticks of celery (tender parts), sliced
5 large cloves of garlic, sliced thick
salt and pepper
1 cup of chopped parsley
a few sprigs of mint
3 tablespoons of oil
1 lemon (optional)

Peel the potatoes and cut them into small cubes. Sprinkle salt, to taste. Heat oil in a frypan, put in the garlic-slices and fry lightly. Remove the garlic and set aside.

Turn down the heat, and put in the potato-cubes with half the parsley. Stir-fry for about fifteen minutes, until the potatoes are cooked through and turn crisp on the outside. Put back the garlic-slices, along with the celery, the rest of the parsley and the shredded mint, and mix. You may squeeze a little lemon over the dish before serving.

Salads, Beans and Vegetables

Serves 4 – 6

Dorate cotolette di melanzane:
Golden Eggplant Cutlets

INGREDIENTS
2 eggplants, *peeled and cut into slices 1 cm thick*
125 g of breadcrumbs
200 g of grated pecorino
3 cloves of garlic, *chopped*
2 tablespoons of chopped parsley
2 eggs
salt and pepper
oil *(for shallow frying)*

Put the eggplant slices in a bowl of salted water.

Sieve the breadcrumbs, then mix them with grated pecorino, half the chopped garlic, some parsley, and salt and pepper.

Beat the eggs in a bowl, and mix them with the rest of the garlic and parsley, adding some salt and pepper.

Take the eggplant slices out and scrape off any seeds remaining on the surface. Dry them.

Dip each slice thoroughly in the egg, making sure that the sides are coated as well. Roll the slice in breadcrumbs, pressing them in so that they cover the whole surface.

Heat oil of about two centimetres depth in a frypan. Keeping the heat low, fry the cutlets four or five at a time, turning them over with tongs until they turn golden brown (approximately five minutes for each side).

Note
There is no need to waste any leftover ingredients. Mix the breadcrumbs with the broken egg, and fry an omelette in the oil left in the frypan. This is called '*Pesce di uovo*' ('egg-fish'), and is often taken on picnics. You may add some ricotta, or some cooked peas or broccoli, to the omelette, and fold it over.

Peperoni e Pomodori Ripieni:
Stuffed Capsicums and Tomatoes

Salads, Beans and Vegetables

Serves 8

Peperoni e pomodori ripieni:
Stuffed Capsicums and Tomatoes

If you face one of those occasions when you have a mixed gathering of vegetarians, meat-eaters, and 'in-betweenies' who like 'just a little meat, thank you', this dish is your salvation. If any dislike capsicum or tomato, egg-plant (page 91) works just as well.

The quantities given are only a guide, and presume that you have three meat-eaters, three 'in-betweenies', and two vegetarians. You will need to adjust the quantity of each filling you prepare, according to the makeup of your gathering.

INGREDIENTS
8 tomatoes, large and firm
6 capiscums (2 red, 2 yellow, 2 green)
1½ cups of uncooked rice
250 g of minced pork
250 g of minced veal
4–6 tablespoons of oil
75 g of butter
6 mushrooms
1 small onion, chopped
2 chopped olives
3 cloves of garlic, chopped
3 tablespoons of chopped parsley
180 g of grated pecorino
salt

Wash the capsicums. Take four of them and cut across the top of each, about two centimetres from the stalk. Set the tops aside to use as lids. Carefully scoop out and discard the pith and seeds. To make sure the capsicums sit well in a baking-tray, take a thin slice off the bottom. (This, by letting the steam in, also enables them to cook through evenly, without losing their colour or shape.)

Cut the remaining two capsicums into halves, then take out and discard the pith and seeds.

Take a slice off the top of the tomatoes, about a centimetre. Scoop out about half the flesh inside. With capsicums and tomatoes together, you should have a total of sixteen shells.

Mix the minced veal with the minced pork in a bowl, adding chopped garlic, two teaspoons of salt, two tablespoons of chopped parsley, and 120 grams of grated pecorino. Put the mix in a frypan and cook slowly for fifteen minutes. Divide into two portions.

Cook the rice in plenty of water, then drain it, rinse, and cool. Divide the cooked rice into two portions.

(see over)

For meat-eaters
Take a little rice from one portion and mix it with one half of the meat-mix. Fill three capiscum-shells and three tomatoes.

For 'in-betweenies'
Mix the leftover meat-mix with what remains from the used portion of rice, and fill three of the capsicum-shells and three tomatoes.

For vegetarians
Over a slow heat, soften the chopped onion in one tablespoon of oil. Add one teaspoon of salt and the chopped mushrooms, chopped olives and parsley, with sixty grams of grated pecorino. Mix in the second portion of rice, and fill two capsicum-shells and two tomatoes.

Arrange all the filled cups with their caps at their side in a large baking dish, and add a cup of water to the dish. Drizzle a little oil over the filled shells, and place a pat of butter on each. Cover the baking-dish with foil and bake in a moderate oven for an hour.

Serves 6 – 8

Roasted Capsicums

INGREDIENTS
4 red capsicums   *salt*
2 tablespoons of olive oil   *pepper*
2 cloves of chopped garlic   *some fresh basil*

Roasting over a gas-flame
Place the capsicums, one at a time, over a full flame and char the skins, turning each one round with a pair of tongs. Do this for about ten minutes, until the capsicum turns black all over. Set aside to cool.

When they are cool enough to handle, remove the charred skin, using a little water, take out pith and seeds, and discard them. Cut the flesh into strips.

Roasting in the oven
Cut the capsicums in halves, and remove their pith and seeds. Place them on a tray in a hot oven, and roast for half an hour or until they become soft. Cool, peel the skin off, and cut into strips.

Finally
Mix olive oil with chopped garlic, salt and pepper, and pour over the capsicums. Sprinkle with chopped basil and serve with bread, or on toast, or with cooked pasta.

Salads, Beans and Vegetables

Serves 4 – 6

Zucchini: Baby Marrow

INGREDIENTS
5 zucchini
cloves of garlic, chopped
salt
2 tablespoons of oil
1 tablespoon of wine vinegar
a pinch of oregano

Wash, dry and trim the zucchini. Cut each in half and slice each half lengthwise into about four thick slices. Dry them.

Heat your oil in a frypan. Put in five or six slices at a time and fry them on a medium heat, sprinkling a little salt. Allow them to cook for five minutes on one side, before turning over for another five minutes. When all the slices are done, return them to the frypan with the chopped garlic, and cook for two to three minutes more. Add vinegar and oregano, and mix well. Serve either warm or cold.

Serves 4

Cipolle dolci col burro:
Sweet Buttered Onions

INGREDIENTS
6 large onions (preferably white), sliced
100 g of butter
3 sticks of celery (tender white parts), sliced
1 cup of chopped parsley
a few sprigs of mint
juice of an orange
1 tablespoon of sugar
salt

Put the onions and butter, with a pinch of salt, into a frypan. Cover and cook slowly for ten minutes. Then transfer to a serving-dish. Heat the orange-juice with sugar for three minutes, then pour it over the onions. Mix-in chopped parsley, sliced celery and shredded mint. The dish is ideal to serve with poultry and game, and it is simply delicious by itself on toast.

Risicato's Sicilian Cookery

Spinaci all'Antonello da Messina

Salads, Beans and Vegetables

Serves 6

Spinaci all' Antonello da Messina

Giuseppe has named this colourful dish after the famous sixteenth century Sicilian painter Antonello da Messina, whose works adorn galleries all over Italy—in Messina, Palermo, Genoa and Syracuse, to name just a few—and can be found in such major international collections as the Metropolitan Museum, New York, the Philadelphia Museum of Art, the Washington National Gallery, the National Gallery, London, the Paris Louvre, and the Kunthistorisches Museum, Vienna. When you finish preparing the dish, you will see why: though simple to make, it offers a painter's palette of brilliant colours, a fitting centre-piece for a dinner party.

INGREDIENTS
3 bunches of spinach*
(**If you use the large-leafed variety grown in Australia, remove the white stems; if you use the softer English spinach, double the quantity*)
1 cup of Napoletana sauce (*see page 21; uses* **400 g of tinned tomatoes**)
4 tablespoons of oil   **2 or 3 cloves of garlic**, *chopped*
4 eggs   **grated pecorino cheese** (*optional*)
salt   **pepper**

Put the spinach into a large saucepan of water, salted and boiling. Cook until the leaves go soft. Drain, cool, and squeeze out excess water. Heat the oil in a large frypan (one that is suitable for serving at table), fry the garlic, add the spinach (seasoning with extra salt, if necessary), and add some pepper. Stir well, breaking up the spinach with a ladle for about ten minutes. Add half the Napoletana sauce (adding the pecorino cheese, if desired), stir well. Turn down the heat. Level the spinach with the back of the ladle. Break the eggs over it. Using a fork, spread egg over the surface of the spinach. Cover and cook on very low heat until the egg is set. Ladle the rest of the Napoletana sauce over the egg to get a good painter's-palette effect.

Penne saltate con gli spinaci
An excellent way to use up any leftovers from *Spinaci all' Antonello* is to mix it with two cups of cooked *penne*-pasta and an extra three tablespoons of Napoletana sauce. Heat some olive oil, and warm the *penne* and spinach through. Sprinkle generously with grated pecorino and serve warm.

All serve 6

Insalata di funghi: Mushroom Salad

INGREDIENTS
*500 g of button mushrooms
(firm and closed)
salt*

*wine vinegar
parsley
juice of half a lemon*

Slice the mushrooms, sprinkle with salt, parsley, a little wine vinegar and lemon juice.

Green Beans with Mushrooms

INGREDIENTS
*500 g of fresh green beans
500 g of button mushrooms
salt*

*3 teaspoons of wine vinegar
2 tablespoons of oil
pepper*

Wash and slice the mushrooms, then mix them with oil, vinegar and a few twists of pepper, and put them in a serving-dish. String, top and tail the green beans. Bring them to the boil in a saucepan of water, then add a little salt. Cook for five to eight minutes until they are cooked but still green. Drain, and add them to the mushrooms, which they will warm through. This dish goes well with crumbed chicken or veal cutlets.

Endive Salad

INGREDIENTS
*3 bunches of endive
salt and pepper*

*olive oil
juice of half a lemon*

Cut the roots off the endives and wash thoroughly, Place them in a large saucepan with water and salt. Bring to the boil, and drain. Season with olive oil, lemon juice and pepper.

Tomato, Cucumber and Basil Salad

INGREDIENTS
*3 large, ripe tomatoes
1 teaspoon of chopped garlic
1 tablespoon of olive oil
basil leaves*

*1 lebanese cucumber
or half a ridge cucumber
salt and pepper
a pinch of oregano*

Slice tomatoes and cucumber. Arrange on a plate and scatter shredded basil leaves over. Mix oil, garlic, oregano, a pinch of salt and pepper, and pour the mixture over.

Preserved Vegetables

Various kinds of preserved vegetables have an important place in Sicilian cuisine, for they take the place of the antipasti *that elsewhere in Italy would normally precede a meal. They are also the normal accompaniments of a friendly glass of wine: Giuseppe remembers his father going to the* taverna *or wine-bar, where along with his drink he would be offered bread, pizza or* inpannata, *perhaps some salami, and the ubiquitous preserved vegetables.*

Preserved Mushrooms

INGREDIENTS
1 kilo of white button mushrooms
1 cup of wine vinegar
4 cloves of garlic
parsley

3 cups of olive oil
2 teaspoons of salt
oregano

Boil two litres of salted water in a large saucepan. Drop in the mushrooms and cook for five minutes. Drain and cool. Half-fill a screwtop jar with mushrooms, and pour the vinegar over. Screw the lid tight, shake well, and leave for an hour. Add oregano, oil and garlic. Make sure the mushrooms are well covered. They will be ready to use in two days.

Preserved Asparagus

Thin asparagus is not suitable for preserving. The asparagus you choose should be green, fleshy, and thick. Stem by stem, cut away any fibrous, hard part; it should be possible to feel it with the cutting-edge of your knife.

Boil plenty of salted water, drop the asparagus stems in, continue boiling for five minutes. Take them out and dry thoroughly in a towel. Put them in a preserving-jar with vinegar (one part), olive oil (three parts), and cloves of garlic, basil, and oregano. Make sure the asparagus is thoroughly submerged, then seal. It should be ready to eat after two weeks.

Preserved Eggplant

Choose firm, shiny, fresh eggplants. peel off the skin, and cut into thick slices. To stop them going brown, drop the slices immediately into plenty of salted water, and soak for an hour. Drain, and dry thoroughly with a cloth. You may keep the slices as they are, or cut them into strips. Put them in a bowl with enough vinegar to cover, and leave for an hour. Remove from the vinegar and put the slices in a preserving-jar with basil, cloves of garlic, and enough olive oil to cover. Make sure the slices are thoroughly submerged, or they will form a mould. Seal. After two weeks, the eggplant is ready to serve, either as an *antipasto* or as a snack on toast.

Olive schiacciate:
Preserved Green Olives

'Schiacciata', 'a quick bash', is the term in Sicily for the treatment handed out to olives that are to be preserved. Giuseppe recommends putting the olives on a towel, folding it over, and administering a firm but light blow sufficient to make a slight split in the olives but not to break or crush them. The knock releases the bitter juices.

Put the split olives in a jar of salted water. Shake it twice a day, and change the salted water every two days for two weeks. After that time, drain the olives and put them in a preserving-jar with one part vinegar and three parts olive oil, enough to cover. Add fresh mint, cloves of garlic, and oregano. Seal. The olives should be ready to eat after five weeks.

Olive nere:
Preserved Black Olives

Black olives need little preparation. Put them straight into a preserving-jar with three parts of oil to one part of vinegar. Seal.

Olive macchiate:
Freshly Picked Black Olives

If you are lucky enough to have access to freshly picked black olives which still have traces of green, they respond well to the following treatment, which is traditional.

Arrange your olives in layers in a cane basket, sprinkling salt between the layers. Place a board or a plate over the top layer, and weight it down with a heavy stone or a brick. The juices should then run out. Replace the salt every two weeks for two months, not forgetting to replace the board and brick also. After two months, you may dry the olives or preserve them in oil and vinegar.

DOLCI

A Venetian Lady

"Sweets to the Sweet"

Serves 6 – 8

Cannoli

INGREDIENTS
500 g plain flour, *sifted*
50 ml of olive oil
beaten egg-white
icing sugar

50 g of sugar
1 egg-yolk
oil, for frying *(not olive oil)*

for the filling
700 g of ricotta cheese
100 ml of orange liqueur

170 g of castor sugar

To make the pastry shells
Make a well in the flour, and in it place sugar, olive oil and egg-yolk. Work in the flour gradually to make a dough. After it has been kneaded for about ten minutes, cover with plastic wrap and chill for an hour.

Roll the pastry out thinly, and cut into rounds approximately 7.5 cm across. Wrap the rounds around metal *cannoli* tubes* and seal the edges with a little egg-white. Be careful to avoid putting egg-white on the metal tube itself, as that will make it very difficult to slip the cooked *cannoli* off, once they are cooked.

Cook the *cannoli* four at a time in heated oil for about one minute, till they are golden brown.

Drain the cooked *cannoli* on kitchen paper for one minute, before you slip them off their metal tubes. Let the pastry cool completely before attempting to fill it. Dust with icing sugar.

To fill the shells
Beat the ricotta and castor sugar together till the mixture becomes fluffy. Then beat in the orange liqueur.

Fill a piping-bag with the mixture and pipe it into the cooked *cannoli* shells.

*Note
If metal *cannoli* moulds are hard to obtain, *cannelloni* pasta shells make an excellent substitute.

Dolci

Serves 6 – 8

Gnoccoli

INGREDIENTS
500 g plain flour
4 eggs
40 ml of oil
125 ml of orange liqueur
oil, for deep frying
icing sugar

Place the flour, eggs, oil and orange liqueur in a bowl, and mix them into a firm dough.

Divide the dough into four sections and roll out each section into a long shape. Then cut each shape into pieces the size of a finger.

Heat your frying oil, and deep-fry the pastry. The *gnoccoli* are cooked when they rise to the surface of the oil. Take them out, and drain them on kitchen paper.

When they have cooled, dust them with icing sugar.

Serves 6 – 8

Casatelli

INGREDIENTS
250 g plain flour
2 eggs
30 g butter
125 ml of white wine
30 ml of water
ricotta cheese
oil, for deep frying
icing sugar

Place the flour, eggs, butter, wine and water in a bowl, and mix into a dough.

Roll the dough out to the thickness of pie pastry, then cut into round shapes with a cutter.

Put small teaspoons of ricotta cheese on one round, cover it with another round, and seal by pressing the edges well together. Repeat till the dough is used up.

Heat the frying oil, and deep fry the *casatelli*. Drain them on kitchen paper.

When they are cool, dust with icing sugar.

Risicato's Sicilian Cookery

Biscotti Vizzinesi

Dolci

Makes 10 large or 20 small biscotti

Biscotti Vizzinesi della Mama Grazia Risicato:

Mama Risicato's Vizzini Biscotti

Mama Risicato's biscotti *had the reputation of being larger than the best sold in Vizzini's colourful Wednesday market. Papa Risicato liked to take them with him to the opera, to share with friends during the interval. They are delicious with coffee, and even better if dipped in a glass of iced* Cinzano, Rosso *or* Bianco.

>INGREDIENTS
>3 cups of self-raising flour
>6 eggs
>6 tablespoons of olive oil
>1 tablespoon of Galliano liqueur
>2 cups of sugar
>zest (grated skin) of 1 lemon

Sift the flour on to a tray or into a mixing-bowl. Make a well in it and break in the eggs. Beat the flour in, a little at a time, either with a fork or using an electric whisk. Pour in the oil as you whisk. When the mixture gets doughy, dust your hands with flour and knead well for ten minutes until you get a soft dough.

Grease two baking-trays. Divide the dough into ten portions, knead them, and roll them into sausage-shapes, each about eight centimetres long. Press along their length with a sharp knife so as to make a cleft. Place the *biscotti* on trays and bake in a very hot oven (fan-forced) for fifteen minutes.

Dissolve two cups of sugar in two cups of water in a large saucepan. Boil slowly over a medium heat for fifteen to twenty minutes to make a thick syrup. Add a little lemon zest, drop in the baked *biscotti*, and stir well so as to coat them with syrup.

Keep turning the *biscotti* until the syrup becomes a sugary coating. Then remove them from the heat, sprinkle the rest of the lemon zest over them, and serve.

Vizzini Backstreet

Dolci

A Note on Dolci
In general, it is not customary to follow main meals with a rich sweet. Instead, Sicilians prefer to eat the fruits that are in season, lightly prepared in a way that enhances their natural flavour. The glorious golden appearance of Pears with Galliano *can be seen in the illustration on page 48. Our* Peaches in White Wine *would have concluded Scarpia's love-feast, if he had lived long enough to enjoy them (page 86).*

Serves 4

Pears with Galliano

INGREDIENTS
4 pears
juice of 1 lemon
2 cups of sugar
a small glass of Galliano

Peel the pears, leaving their stems on. Place them in a saucepan, pouring in three cups of water. Add one and a half cups of sugar, lemon juice, and the *Galliano* liqueur. Simmer gently for half an hour. Cool, then refrigerate. Sprinkle some sugar on the pears before serving

Serves 6

Strawberries sambuca

INGREDIENTS
500 g of strawberries
1 glass of sambuca
4 tablespoons of sugar

Wash the strawberries, remove any stalks, and slice the fruit. Sprinkle sugar and pour a glass of *sambuca* over them. Chill, and serve with ice-cream.

Serves 4

Peaches in White Wine

INGREDIENTS
4 fresh peaches, ripe yet firm
2 glasses of white wine
6 tablespoons of sugar
½ glass of Cinzano Bianco

Cut the peaches into neat segments, and arrange them in a shallow dish. Sprinkle sugar, pour the wine over, and also the *Cinzano*. Cover and refrigerate for two hours. Serve on its own (cream or ice-cream are liable to distort the delicate liqueur-flavour of this sweet).

Risicato's Sicilian Cookery

Light over Vizzini

INDEX

A
Anchovies 5, 22, 33, 73
Angels's Hair Pasta with Asparagus 31
Artichokes 29, **89**
Artichokes in Foil 89
Asparagus 31, 92, **103**
Asparagus and Angels' Hair 31
Asparagus, in eggplant roll 92
Asparagus, Preserved 103

B
Baked Garfish 49
Baked Swordfish 54
Baked Knuckles of Veal 71
Barramundi in Lemon-Butter Sauce 51
Barramundi alla siciliana 50–1
Basil 5, 13, 21, 22, 30, 71, 73, 98, 102
Beans (notes on cooking) 88
Beans, *Borlotti* 5, **13**
Beans, Broad 5, 9, 14, 15, **53**, 88
Beans, Broad: Purée of 9
Beans, Broad: Soup 14, **15**
Beans, Broad: with Mussels 53, 88
Beans, *Fagioli* 5, **13**, 88
Beans, *Fagioli conditi* **13**
Beans, Green 15, **102**
Beans, Green: with Mushrooms 102
Beef, minced 21
Beefsteak Bellini 73
Beefsteak with Mushrooms 86
Beef Stew 64
Bird's Nest 31
Biscotti 109
Bistecca Bellini 73
Bistecca ai funghi 86
Blue-eyed cod 18
Bolognese Sauce 21, 23
Brandy, Prawns in 45
Broad Beans 5, **9**, **14**, 15, **53**, 88
Broad Beans Purée 9
Broad Beans Soup 14
Broccoli **15, 22**, 33, 36
Broccoli Soup 15
Broccoli and Tomato Sauce 22
Brodino 17
Brodo di pollo 17

C
Calamari fritti 47
Calamari ripieni 47
Cannelloni, Meat 25
Cannelloni, Spinach and Ricotta 39
Cannoli 106
Cannoli di ricotta 38, 40
Capelli di angeli ed asparagi 31
Capretto al forno coi funghi 80, **81**
Capretto Vermouth 76
Capretto alla siciliana 82, **83**
capsicum 13, 36, 56, 73, 93, **97**, **98**
Capsicum, Roasted 98
Capsicum, Stuffed 97
Carciofi al cartoccio 89
Casatelli 107
Cassata di ricotta 38, **40**
Cauliflower Salad 51
Celery 8, 9, 11, 13, 14, 15, 17, **54**, 57, **61**, 75, 94, 99
Celery with Buttered Onions 61, 99
Celery with Crisped Potatoes 54, 94
Champagne Duck 61
Chicken Cutlets 62
Chicken in *frittata* 36
Chicken Livers 67
Chicken *Sambuca* 56
Chicken *Siciliana* 21, **57**
Chicken Soup 17
Chicken *Spezzatino* 64
Chicken Stew 64
Chickpea Soup 14
Cinzano 5, 40, **60**, 76, 111
Cinzano with Milk-fed Goat or **Lamb 76**
Cinzano with Spatchcock 60
Cipolle calabresi 88
Cipolle dolci coi burro 99
Coniglio Verga 75
Costate di maiale ripiene 70
Cozze con fave fresche 52, **53**
Cucuzza 13, 88
Cuttlefish with Black Spaghetti 27
Cuttlefish, cleaning of 27

D
Dorate cotolette di melanzane 95
Duck, Champagne 61

E
'Eggfish' 95
Eggplant **30**, **91**, 92, **93**, **95**, **103**

Risicato's Sicilian Cookery

Eggplant Cutlets 95
Eggplant, Fried 92
Eggplant, Parmigiana 93
Eggplant, Preserved 103
Eggplant Rolls 92
Eggplant, Stuffed 91
Eggplant in Tomato Sauce 93
Eggs, *frittata* 36
Eggs in Napoletana Sauce 17, 36
Endive Salad 102

F

Fagioli 5, **13**, 88
Fagioli conditi 13
Fave fresche 14, 53, 88
Fave fresche, cozze con 53
Fave fresche, minestra con 14
Fegatini di pollo 67
Fennel with Spaghetti and Walnuts 29
Fish: Barramundi 50, 51
      Garfish 45, 49
      Garfish, Fried or Baked 49
      Sardines, Fried 53
      Soup 18
      Swordfish 54
      Tuna 5, 31, 35, 73, 91
Fried: *Calamari* 47
      Cannoli 106
      Casatelli 107
      Chicken Cutlets 62
      Eggplant 92
      Garfish 49
      Gnoccoli 107
      Meat-Patties 67
      Ricotta 39
      Sardines 53
      Veal cutlets 62
      Zucchini 99
Frittata 21, 36

G

Galetto arrosto 59
Galetto con Cinzano 60
Galliano 5, 40, 109, **111**
Gamberi Costa 45
Garfish, Fried or Baked 49
Gnoccoli 107
Goat with Vermouth 76
Goat, Roasted with Mushrooms 81
Goat *Siciliana* 83
Green beans 15, 62; **with Mushrooms** 102

I–K

Inpannata 33
Insalata di funghi 102
Insalata di mare 43
Involtini di melanzane 92
Kidney beans (see *Fagioli*) 5

L

Lamb 11, **76, 81, 83**
Lamb, Baked with Mushrooms 81
Lamb *Siciliana* 83
Lamb with Vermouth 76
Lasagna 5, 23, 24
Lasagna, Meat 23
Lasagna, Seafood 24
Lentils, brown 5, 11
Lentil Soup, Non-Vegetarian 11
Lentil Soup, Vegetarian 11
Linguine 5, 20, 22, 29, 44
Livers, Chicken 67

M

Macaroni *(Maccheroni)* 20
Macco 9
Maiale, costate di 70
Maiale ripieno 68, 69
Marinara 18, 24, 43, **44**
Marinara, Lasagna 24
Marinara, spaghetti di 44
Marinara, zuppa alla 18
Marrow 13
Marsala 5, 40, 66
Meat: beef 21, 23, 64, 73, 86
Meat: chicken 17, 36, 56, 57, 62, 64
Meat: chicken livers 67
Meat: duck 61
Meat: lamb 76, 81, 83
Meat: milk-fed goat 76, 79, 81, 83
Meat: pork 13, 25, 69, 70, 97
Meat: quail 59
Meat: rabbit 75
Meat: spatchcock 59, 60
Meat: tripe 85
Meat: veal 15, 17, 21, 23, 25, 62, 64, 65, 66, 67, 71, 97
Meat-Balls in Soup 17
Meat-Patties 67
Melanzane (eggplant) 30, **91, 92, 93, 95, 103**
Melanzane, cotolette di 95
Melanzane, fritte 92
Melanzane, involtini di 92

Index

Melanzane alla Parmigiana 93
Melanzane, Preserved 103
Melanzane ripiene 91
Minestra di ceci 14
Minestra con fave fresche 14
Minestra coi piselli 8
Minestra tutte le verdure col vitello 15
Minestrone 13
Mixed Vegetable Soup with Veal 15
Mushrooms 31, 35, **70**, 81, **86, 89**, 97, **102**, **103**
Mushrooms, Preserved 103
Mushroom Risotto 69–70
Mussels, cleaning of 42
Mussels 18, 42, 43, **50, 53**
Mussels with Broad Beans 53

N–O

Napoletana Sauce 14, 21, 23, 24, 2**5**, **27, 29**, 30, 35, 36, 47, 66, 69, 93, 101
Napoletana Sauce, Eggs in 36
Octopus, cleaning of 42
Octopus 43
Olives 5, 13, 69, 75, 97, **104**
Olive macchiate 104
Olive nere 104
Olive schiacciate 104
Olives, Preserved 104
Onions, Sweet Buttered 99
Ossobuco 71

P

Pappardelle 25
Pasta, notes on cooking 20
Pasta with Artichokes 29
Pasta with Asparagus 31
Pasta: *Cannelloni* 25
Pasta: *Cannelloni*, Spinach/Ricotta 39
Pasta: *Lasagna* 23
Pasta: *Lasagna*, Seafood 24
Pasta: *Linguine* 5, 20, 22, 29, 44
Pasta: *Pappardelle* 25
Pasta: *Penne* 5, 38, **101**
Pasta: *Penne* **with Ricotta 38**
Pasta: *Penne saltate con gli spinaci* **101**
Pasta: *Spaghetti* 5, 21, **22, 27, 29**, **30, 44, 57**, 65
Pasta: *Spaghetti in bianco* 21, **57**, 65
Pasta: *Spaghetti* **with Cuttlefish 27**
Pasta: *Spaghetti* **with Eggplant 30**
Pasta with Fennel and Walnut 29
Pasta: *Spaghetti alla marinara* **44**
Pasta: *Spaghetti alla Norma* **30**

Pasta: Spaghetti with Seafood Mix 44
Pasta, Sauces for 21–22, 27–29
Pastina 5, 8, 14, 17
Peas **8**, 15, 35, 64, 76
Pea Soup 8
Peaches in White Wine 111
Pears with Galliano 111
Penne with Ricotta 38
Penne saltata con spinaci **101**
Peppers (capsicum) 13, 36, 56, 73, 93, **97, 98**
Peperoni e pomodori ripieni 97
Peppers, roasted 98
Peppers, stuffed 97
Pescatore, risotto di 44
Pesce di uovo 95
Pesce Spada 54
Pesce, stracciatella di 18
Pigeon 17
Pig's trotters 13
Piselli **Soup 8**
Pizza 33, 103
Pollo agrodolce con sambuca 56
Pollo alla siciliana 57
Pollo, brodo di 17
Polpette alla Palmina 67
Pomodori ripieni 97
Pork 13, 25, **69**, **70**, 97
Pork Chops, Stuffed 70
Pork Steaks, Stuffed 69
Pork, minced 25, 97
Potato 8, 13, 17, 36, 54, 56, 57, 61, 64, 65, 66, 76, 81, 83, 85, **94**
Potatoes, Crisped with Celery 54, **94**
Potato Soup 8
Prawns 18, cleaning 42, 43, 44, **45**
Prawns, Brandied 45
Preserved Asparagus 103
Preserved Eggplants 103
Preserved Mushrooms 103
Preserved Olives 104

Q–R

Quail, Baked 59
Rabbit Verga 75
Rice 5, 17, 35, 44, 47, 64, 69, 70
Rice, Fisherman's 44
Ricotta 38, 39, 40, 106, 107
Ricotta, cannoli di 38, **40**, **106**
Ricotta, cassata di 38, **40**
Ricotta fritta 39
Ricotta, with *penne* **38**

Ricotta and Spinach Canneloni 39
Risotto 21, 35, 44, 47, 64, **69–70**
Risotto, Mushroom 69–70
Risotto di pescatore 44
Risotto Risicato 35
Roasted Capsicums 98
Roast Spatchcock 59
Roast Veal 65

S

Sambuca 5, **56**, 111
Sambuca, Chicken 56
Sambuca with Strawberries 111
Sardines, Fried 53
Sauce, *Aglio-Olio* 22
Sauce, *Bolognese* 21
Sauce, Broccoli and Tomato 22
Sauce, Garlic and Olive Oil 22
Sauce, *Napoletana* 21
Seafood 18, 24, 42, 43, 44
Seafood, *Lasagna* 24
Seafood Platter 43, 44
Seafood Soup 18
Soup with Broad Beans 9, 14
Soup, Broccoli 15
Soup, Chicken 17
Soup, Chickpea 14
Soup, *Fagioli* 13
Soup, Fish 18
Soup, Lentil (Non-Vegetarian) 11
Soup, Lentil (Vegetarian) 11
Soup with Meat-Balls 17
Soup, Mixed Vegetable with Veal 15
Soup, Pea 8
Soup, Potato 8
Soup, Seafood 18
Spada, Pesce 54
Spaghetti 5, 21, 22, **27**, 29, **30**, **44**, 57, 65
Spaghetti in bianco 21, 57, 65
Spaghetti with Cuttlefish 27
Spaghetti with Eggplant 30
Spaghetti alla marinara 44
Spaghetti alla Norma 30
Spaghetti with Seafood Mix 44
Spaghetti con le seppie 26, 27
Spatchcock 17, **59**, 60
Spatchcock with Cinzano 60
Spatchcock, Roast 59
Spezzatino, Beef 64
Spezzatino, Chicken 17, 64
Spezzatino di pollo 17, 64

Spinach 15, 33, 36, **39**, **101**
Spinaci all' Antonello da Messina 101
Spinaci, penne saltate con gli 101
Spinach and Ricotta *Cannelloni* 39
Squid, cleaning 42; cooking 43
Squid, Fried 47
Squid, Stuffed 47
Steak, Bellini 73
Steak with Mushrooms 86
Stew, Beef 64
Stew, Chicken 64
Stracciatella di pesce 18
Strawberries in Sambuca 111
Swordfish, Baked 54

T

Three-in-One Winter Fare 13
Tomatoes 5, 8, 11, 13, 14, 15, 17, 18, **21**, 22,
    23, 25, 27, 30, 31, 33, 35, **36**, 47, 57, 64,
    69, 71, 75, 83, 85, 93, **97**, 101, **102**
Tomato and Cucumber Salad 102
Tomatoes, Stuffed 97
Tripe, San Gregorio 85
Trippa pa Festa 85
Tuna 5, 31, 35, 73, 91

V–Z

Veal 15, 17, 21, 23, 25, **62**, 64, **65**, **66**, 67, **71**, 97
Veal chops 15
Veal Cutlets 62
Veal fillets 62, 66
Veal Knuckles 71
Veal, minced 17, 21, 25, 67, 97
Veal, *Ossobuco* 71
Veal, Pink 66
Veal, Roast 65
Veal shanks 64
Veal, White 66
Vermicelli 20, **31**
Vermouth—see Cinzano
Vitello bianco 66
Vitello rosa 66
Vitello 15, 17, 21, 23, 25, **62**, 64, **65**, **66**, 67, **71**, 97
Vitello al forno 65
Walnut, Spaghetti with Fennel 29
Wine, red 69
Wine, white 5, 17, 27, 35, 43, 44, 57, 65, 66,
    71, 81, 111
Zampe di maiale 13
Zucchini 15, **36**, 61, **99**
Zuppa alla marinara 18